Babycare

ams

CARROLL & BROWN PUBLISHERS LIMITED

This revised edition first published
in the United Kingdom in 2006 by
Carroll & Brown Publishers Limited,
20 Lonsdale Road, London, NW6 6RD

Copyright © Carroll & Brown Limited 1996, 2002 and 2006

Previously published under the title *Babycare for Beginners*

A CIP catalogue record for this book is available from the British Library

ISBN 1-904760-29-5

10987654321

Reproduced by RALI, Bilbao, Spain
Printed and bound in Spain by Bookprint

CONTENTS

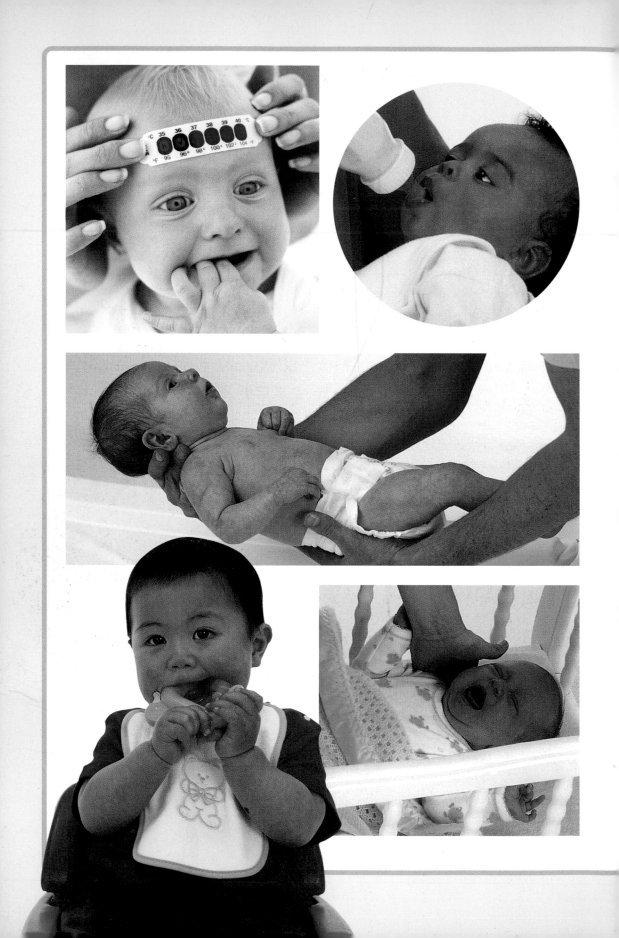

FOREWORD

Taking care of a baby is round-the-clock work and a hands-on occupation, and once a baby arrives, all parents suddenly realize exactly what it means to "have their hands full"! Having been carried around for the first nine months of their lives, babies yearn to be in constant contact with their caregivers. Rare is the parent who very shortly doesn't wish he or she had an extra pair of hands when it comes to taking care of a baby, particularly at such nerve-racking times as getting a baby bathed and dressed.

Now help is at hand for new parents and others unfamiliar with basic babycare. In *Babycare* you'll find everything you need to know in order to hold, feed, carry, change, dress, bathe, soothe and comfort a newborn baby up to his or her first birthday. With special sections on getting out and about with your baby, common skin conditions found in young babies and essential items of clothing for a newborn, and answers to the most frequently asked questions on feeding and weaning, soothing a crying baby and sleep, there is also very useful information on immunization schedules and first aid.

Large step-by-step photographs illustrate all the stages of the essential care routines such as changing a nappy, putting on a jumpsuit, using a baby carrier or preparing a bottle. Short, concise captions make following the steps easy – even at a distance. And when you do have more time, there is a great deal of useful information to consider.

Having shown the early stages of the book to the parents of older children in my practice, the overwhelming reaction has been "We wish this book had been around when we first had our babies!" I know what they mean. Parenting skills are not inborn, they have to be acquired. I hope this book helps new parents, grandparents, babysitters and caregivers gain the confidence and competence necessary not only to care for their babies but to enjoy doing so.

Your marvellous newborn

At birth, all your baby's senses are intact and ready to be used. Immediately after birth your baby can see you quite well, but her focus is best at 20–25 cm. Your baby will enjoy watching you and will track your movements for short periods. Newborns hear very well. You may notice your baby turns towards you when you speak or sing – she recognizes your voice from when she was in the uterus. She won't like loud noises, but may be calmed by low-pitched sounds such as the washing machine.

Babies seem able to distinguish certain flavours from birth and, likewise, have pronounced smell preferences, being able to distinguish their own mother's milk from that of another mother's. And, of course, all newborns have a highly developed sense of touch. Cuddles and skin-to-skin contact are highly reassuring and soothing as well as being important in developmental terms.

Your baby is also born with a number of important automatic responses – reflexes that are thought to help babies with their basic needs. Many of these early reflexes will slowly disappear over the first six months.

Your baby's reflexes

THE SUCKING REFLEX
This is your baby's natural instinct to suck on whatever is put in her mouth. She'll suck readily on your nipple, on the teat of a bottle, or on your finger. This reflex is crucial for survival, and a strong suck is a sign of a healthy baby. Your baby may also suck her fingers or thumb to soothe herself.

THE ROOTING REFLEX
If you tickle the side of your baby's cheek she will turn towards you and try to suck on your finger. This reflex helps a baby find food. It can help to tickle your baby's lips when you're encouraging her to feed.

THE GRASPING REFLEX
If you place your finger in your baby's hand she'll grasp it tightly. This grasp can be so strong that you could almost lift her up by her arms.

THE STARTLE OR MORO REFLEX
This occurs when your baby hears a loud noise or is moved suddenly. During the startle, your baby's hands will suddenly go out to her sides with her fingers spread. Then she'll bring her arms back into her chest with clenched fists, and probably end this with a crying episode.

THE WALKING OR STEPPING REFLEX
This occurs if you hold your baby upright under her arms and let her feet touch a flat surface. She'll naturally make stepping movements and try to move forward.

DIVING REFLEX
Although you should never leave your baby to swim under water, if you place your newborn under water for a short while, she'll swim happily. This is because her lungs automatically seal off under water.

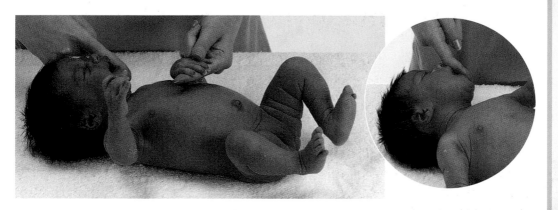

ROOTING

If you stroke your baby's cheek or the area around her mouth, her head will turn in the direction of the stroking and her lips will search for a nipple or teat. This continues while the baby is nursing.

GRASPING

The grasp reflex is triggered by stroking your baby's hands or pressing the balls of her feet at the base of her toes. Your baby's fingers curl as if to hold an object, or her toes curl. This reflex usually disappears after about 4 months.

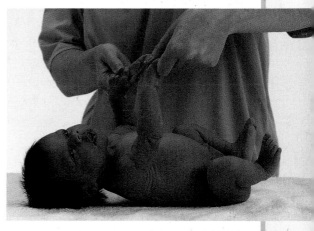

STARTLE

Sudden changes in light, noise levels, movement or position can trigger this reflex, as can your baby's own muscle twitches during sleep. The startle reflex stays with us all to a certain extent, but you will find that by the time your baby is six months old, she'll experience it less.

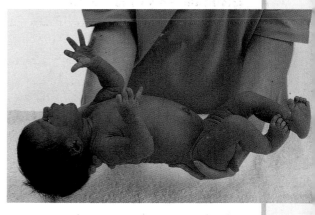

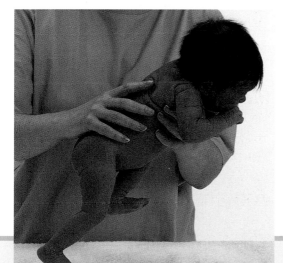

WALKING

If you hold your baby in a standing position, she will lift each foot in turn, as if trying to walk. This reflex usually disappears by the time your baby is two months old.

HANDLING YOUR BABY

You will be picking up and carrying your baby a great deal during the first few months and this should always be done gently and smoothly so as not to frighten him. Though a baby is usually more robust than you might think, it's important never to handle your baby roughly or shake him. When picking up your baby always hold him close, make reassuring noises and support his head.

Picking up from a face-up position

If your baby is sleeping it is a good idea to rouse him gently before lifting. Until you become practised at lifting, your baby may find the motion rather startling, which can cause him to cry. Talking to your baby softly or gently stroking his cheek as you prepare to pick him up will help to reassure him. To make it easy on your back, always bend down close to your baby before lifting him up.

When laying your baby down, simply reverse these instructions, easing him gently away from your body, while supporting his head and neck with one hand and his bottom with the other.

BACK CARE
As your baby gets older – and heavier – make sure you bend down close to him when you pick him up or lay him down so the strain on your back is minimized.

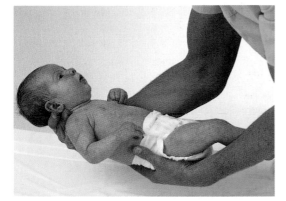

1 SUPPORT HIS NECK AND BOTTOM

Lean in close to your baby and slide one hand under his head and neck and the other beneath his bottom. A few calm words from you will reassure him and give him a sense of security.

2 GENTLY BEGIN TO LIFT HIM

Still leaning well forward, take your baby's weight in your hands, making sure his head is well supported. Talk to him and establish eye contact as you raise him smoothly from the surface. Try to keep his head raised slightly above the level of the rest of his body.

3 REST HIM IN THE CROOK OF YOUR ARM

As you bring him close to your chest, slide the hand supporting his bottom up to support his head as well. Bend your other arm across your body so that you can support his head in the crook of your elbow and his body along the length of this arm. Use your other hand for extra support.

Picking up from a face-down position

Most of the time you will be picking up a young baby from a face-up or supine position, as this is the safest position for your baby to lie in. However, there will be rare occasions when you have to pick your baby up from a face-down or prone position, for instance when he rolls forward during sleep, which is likely to happen more and more often as he gets older.

Initially, you may find this manoeuvre awkward, but with experience it will soon feel natural. The guidelines provided should give you confidence in your technique.

As with all lifting manoeuvres, take care to make it easy on your back. Changing tables, cots, mattresses and baby baths should all be about waist level, which will make your movements both safer and more comfortable. Bend your knees, not your back.

Your older baby

By about six months of age your baby should become quite adept at rolling from his back on to his front. So, even if you lay him down on his back, he may turn over and you will have to pick him up later from a face-down position.

By this age, too, he will also have mastered the skill of raising his head and chest off a surface. You might like to put him in a face-down position (and therefore pick him up from this position) to enable him to further strengthen his neck muscles. Playing airplanes – stretching out your arms and getting him to copy you – can be fun for both of you.

CAUTION

The wrong way to pick him up

When you support a young baby's neck, make sure you keep his head in line with the rest of his body. Don't raise his head further back than the rest of his body or press too hard on his neck – you may restrict his breathing.

1 SUPPORT HER NECK AND TUMMY WITH YOUR HANDS

Slide one hand between your baby's legs until your palm rests on her chest. Gently position your other hand underneath her cheek, making sure her head is well supported.

2 LIFT AND TURN HER TOWARDS YOU

Slowly raise your baby up, making sure her body weight is well supported. As you lift her up, gently rotate her towards your own body. Keep her head raised slightly above the rest of her body, supporting her head with the crook of your arm.

3 CRADLE HER IN YOUR ARM

As you turn her towards you, put the hand you had between her legs underneath her bottom. Lower your other arm so your baby's head rests in the crook of your elbow, and your forearm supports her along her length.

Holding your baby

All babies enjoy physical contact; in fact they need to be held and caressed to feel secure and loved. As a new parent you will find yourself holding your baby for a great deal of her waking hours.

Your newborn will want to be held close to you. She has only recently emerged from the confined space of your uterus so she will feel happier and more comfortable if she is gently, but securely, held in your arms with her limbs kept close to her body.

For your part, holding your baby will give you the opportunity to watch as her expressions change and she discovers more about the world around her.

Until your baby can hold her head up independently, you will need to be careful to support her neck whenever you lift or hold her.

Your older baby

Once your baby has gained sufficient control over her neck and can assume an upright head posture, at around three months, she will require less support. There are a number of ways to carry your baby so that she can get a different view of her surroundings.

HOLDING A YOUNGER BABY

FACE DOWN IN YOUR ARMS
Your baby's head should be supported by the crook of
your arm, with your forearm supporting the length of his
body. Put your other arm between his legs so that your
hand is resting on his tummy.

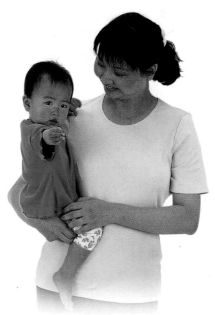

NESTLED AGAINST YOUR SHOULDER
A baby will be
comforted if he is in a
position where he can
feel your pulse or hear
your heartbeat. Use one
hand to support your
baby's bottom and the
other to protect his neck.

HOLDING AN OLDER BABY

FRONT FACING FORWARDS
Hold your baby
with her back
against you, with
one arm under her
arm and your hand
across her chest. Use
your other hand to
support her bottom.

ON YOUR HIP
Sit your baby astride your hip with her
legs either side of your body and support
her with one arm under her bottom. Use
your free hand for extra support on her
back if she can't hold on sufficiently.

Carrying your baby

Whether you are taking your baby for a local outing or wanting to keep him in close proximity at all times, an infant carrier is the ideal choice. Using one of the many types available, you will be free to move around and use your hands to perform everyday tasks while your baby will feel safe and snug. Soft cloth carriers are ideal for young babies, while older or heavier babies are best carried in more substantial backpacks with aluminium frames.

CHOOSING A CARRIER

Cotton, padded and machine washable baby carriers are one of the most popular ways of transporting a young baby. Most models enable you to hold your baby either close to your chest or facing forwards. A young baby will be reassured by the sound of your heartbeat; an older baby will enjoy looking out at new surroundings.

Baby carriers are sold according to your baby's age or with a maximum weight level. They have stiff padding behind the head to give extra support and protection to a young baby who doesn't yet have strong enough muscles to hold up his head on his own. For forward-facing use with an older baby, this padding is often removable. After washing, make sure that all fastenings remain secure.

It is very easy for a young baby to overheat inside a snug, padded carrier as he is held close against an adult's chest. Be sure to dress your baby in light clothing, especially in the summer months. Check every now and then that your baby is not sweating too much or in any discomfort. If he is, carefully remove him from the carrier to a suitably safe spot. Take off the carrier and attend to his needs.

ADJUSTABLE STRAPS
A baby carrier with adjustable straps mean that it can be used comfortably by either parent.

14

There are many baby carriers on the market, so choose one that will best suit your needs, whether it's to carry your baby around the house, or for longer trips away from home.

- The carrier should fit you comfortably and hold your baby securely.

- Look for wide, well-padded shoulder and back straps that will help to distribute the weight so the straps are less likely to dig in.

- It should be easy to put on and adjust. You must be able to get the baby in and out of it without help.

- Look for adequate head support for babies under four months old. The carrier should give good support for the baby's head, neck and back.

- Make sure the baby cannot slip through the gaps in the sides and check that the carrier's leg holes are well padded.

- Only buy a machine washable, shrink-proof carrier that has the British Standard label.

PERFECT FOR SMALLER BABIES
This small, lightweight but well-padded baby carrier is great for newborns and smaller babies. It envelopes your baby close to you but is less cumbersome than some other makes.

COMFORT
The popular Wilkinet carrier is heralded as one of the most comfortable. Just make sure you read the fitting instructions to make sense of all the straps before putting it on. Your baby can be placed front facing in, out, back or hip.

Getting your baby in and out of a baby carrier

Carrying your baby in a carrier has many advantages. You will be able to go about your daily tasks while keeping your baby close. It allows you to have constant contact with him so that you can caress and talk to him and offer reassurance when needed. Your baby will enjoy this feeling of closeness and will take pleasure from the feel of your body and the sound of your voice. In fact, the majority of parents say that they feel much closer to their babies and more 'complete' when they practise 'baby wearing'.

Bear in mind that no matter how much support the carrier provides, you should always protect your baby's head with your hands when bending forward or to the side. A young baby up to four months of age will also need to have his neck well supported, which is why most carriers have some form of headrest.

For safety's sake, always put the carrier on and make sure it is securely fastened before you put your baby inside it; similarly, remove your baby from the carrier to a safe place before taking it off. Never leave your baby unattended in the carrier. Don't use the carrier to carry your baby while you are driving or as an outer wrap for your baby.

1 **PUT THE CARRIER ON FIRST**
Following the manufacturer's instructions, fasten the straps and the buckles. When you feel comfortable and the carrier is secure, pick up your baby.

2 Ease your baby inside
Sit down comfortably on a chair and open out the carrier. Holding your baby under his armpits, slowly lift him into the carrier.

3 Adjust the straps
Once he's comfortably seated, check that your baby's weight is evenly supported and adjust the straps accordingly.

4 Removing your baby from a carrier
When you are ready to take your baby out of the carrier, sit down, loosen the straps then lean forwards as you lift him out.

Out and about with your baby

It's never too soon to include your baby in your outings as long as you take certain precautions. It is a good idea to avoid crowds and rush hour times, where you may be jostled, and exposing your baby to people who may be ill.

There is no special age your baby needs to be before you can take her outdoors, as long as you are well prepared and your baby is well dressed. Your baby can't fully regulate her body temperature so always dress her in one more layer of clothing than what you would wear in the same environment, and keep a check on her temperature to make sure she isn't too cold or too hot.

On the move

SLINGS AND CARRIERS

These are great for young babies because they love to be close to you and you have your hands free to do other things. They can put strain on your back as your baby gets older, but used correctly (see Getting your baby in and out of a baby carrier, pages 16–17), slings and carriers can give you the freedom to get out and about without having to take the car or heft the pushchair around.

PUSHCHAIRS

There are so many different pushchairs available now that you might find it difficult to choose! Think carefully about your individual needs before buying a pushchair. Will you be using public transport often or will you have to lift it into the back of the car? Do you live at the end of a rutted farm track or in the middle of town? Also, think about where you are going to store the pushchair when it's not in use.

CAR TRAVEL

You will need a car seat to get your baby home from hospital, so this will be an important first purchase. The first car seat you will need will be a rear-facing, portable car seat that can be removed from the

PACK A HAT

No matter what the weather, a hat is a vital piece of travel kit. A great deal of heat is lost through an uncovered head in cold weather; and in the heat a hat will help to protect your baby against sunburn.

car and used as a carrier, chair or rocker, or one that comes as part of a pushchair travel system. Babies should ride in these rear-facing seats for as long as possible, at least until around age nine months to a year. Infant car seats are best placed on the rear seat, but some are suitable for the front passenger side, providing there is no air bag fitted. When buying a car seat, make sure it fits in your car with minimal movement and that it is padded against side impacts.

FEEDING ON THE MOVE

Travelling with a breastfed baby is much easier than with a bottlefed one. A breastfeeding mother doesn't have to worry about packing bottles and formula or sterilizing all the equipment. Your milk is always ready – and always at the right temperature. Also, the comfort of nursing can reduce the stress of being in unfamiliar places.

If you are bottlefeeding, there are a variety of ready-to-feed formulas that are very convenient additions to your travel kit.

REAR-FACING CAR SEATS

Buying the right seat is critical, so make sure you know all there is to know about the type of car seat that fits in your car and how it is properly secured.

SAFE DINING

There are several portable seats and devices to hold your baby safely and comfortably on almost any chair when dining out in restaurants – not every restaurant has baby chairs.

Soothing a crying baby

During the first few weeks of life, crying is the only way your baby can communicate his needs. Most commonly, a baby cries because he is hungry but a number of other situations – discomfort, loneliness and boredom – will trigger this response (see right). A regular caregiver will soon learn to recognize the different cries that can indicate the various causes, but sometimes your baby will cry for no discernible reason. This will no doubt upset and frustrate even the most confident parent, but remember, don't take your baby's crying personally; simply comfort and reassure him with your presence.

It is important that you respond to your young baby's cries within a few minutes. The longer you leave your baby to cry, the more distressed he will become, making it more difficult for you to interpret the original source of his anxiety.

Babies whose cries are ignored become non-responsive as they mature. Be reassured: you won't spoil your baby if you respond to his cries. You will, however, communicate to him that his needs matter to you and that

SOOTHING WAYS

Babies respond differently to various soothing methods. Here are a few things that might just help to sooth your crying baby:

- Rocking a baby against your shoulder or on your lap can calm the most excitable baby.

- Rhythmic bottom patting, usually accompanied with a rocking motion, will further relax him.

- Use your voice to calm your baby. Your baby loves to hear your voice – talking or singing. Find the particular tone or pitch that best calms your baby.

- Swing your baby in a hammock or suspended baby seat. Alternatively, you could lie in a hammock with your baby in your arms and sway gently.

- Turn the lights down and introduce a low, monotonous sound such as the hum from a fan or household machine.

they will be met. If your baby cries a lot and there are times when you find it hard to cope, ask your health visitor for help.

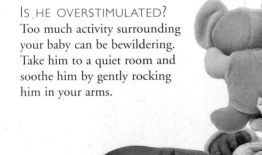

IS HE OVERSTIMULATED?
Too much activity surrounding your baby can be bewildering. Take him to a quiet room and soothe him by gently rocking him in your arms.

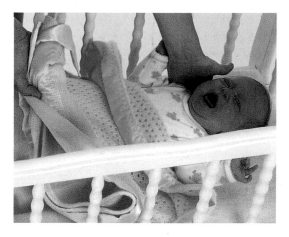

Is she too hot or cold?

A young baby can quickly overheat or chill because her body's temperature control system takes months to become fully operational. Check her temperature or feel the back of her neck or her tummy. If she is too cold, add a layer. If too hot, remove a blanket or a layer of her clothing.

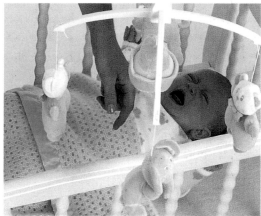

Offering a dummy

Fretful babies are often comforted by sucking, so offering a dummy for short periods of time can be soothing. A dummy is no substitute for a parent's love and attention, so try to limit its use to calming stressful situations and before sleep. A dummy must always be kept sterile and it should never be sweetened or tied around your baby's neck.

Is she bored?

Your baby may need something to interest her. Even a small baby may stop crying if you give her a toy to play with or a mobile to distract her.

Is he lonely?

Most babies don't enjoy being separated from their parents. If you cannot constantly be in the same room as your baby, return frequently, turn on some gentle, soothing music or talk to him loudly so he knows you are nearby.

Your crying baby

Crying is a newborn baby's primary method of communicating with you – of telling you that something is wrong, be it hunger, tiredness, a nappy change or even boredom. After a while you will come to recognize the different sorts of cries your baby makes, but for many people in the early days of parenthood, persistent crying can be very distressing.

Q **My baby is very quiet and placid. He whimpers now and again, usually because he's hungry, but most of the time he is very quiet. Most other new mums I talk to seem to go through hell with their baby's regular crying fits. Is there something wrong with my son?**

A There's no reason whatsoever to think that there's something wrong with your baby just because he doesn't seem to cry as much as others. Some babies are just built that way, and with luck he will hold on to that even temperament throughout childhood and adolescence! Also, this could be a matter of perception: some mothers just can't stand any amount of crying, while others simply feel less stressed by it and know that it's a natural response in all babies. If you are really worried that your son is unnaturally quiet, talk to your health visitor or visit your doctor for a checkup.

Q **My newborn baby seems to cry for no apparent reason and I don't seem to be able to comfort her. What can I do?**

A One of your first tasks as a new parent will be to find out why your baby cries and how you can comfort her. Most of the time addressing her basic needs – food, a dry nappy, entertainment or sleep – will do the trick. Most babies go through a fussy period every day (often at the same time every day) when it seems as if nothing you do will help. Often, playing quiet music, a quick outing in the fresh air or a drive in the car might do the trick. If your baby cries inconsolably in the early evening and she is between three and 14 weeks old, it may be that she is suffering from colic, for which there is no full medical explanation or proven cure. You have to trust your own instincts: if nothing you do is having any effect and you do not think she is suffering from colic, express your concerns to your doctor or health visitor.

Q I find my baby's tears so stressful that I have to walk away from her when she cries for long periods. Are there any things I can do that will help me?

A As long as you ensure that your baby is safe before you walk away from her, you are probably doing the right thing. Many mothers experience these feelings, and walking away gives you time to overcome the anxiety and regain your composure. If you can, ask your partner or another adult to step in and try to calm your baby, or telephone someone close to you for emotional support. Also, talk to other mums to find out how they cope – you may be surprised at just how many parents go through this.

Q What's the current advice on using dummies to pacify a crying baby?

A The sucking reflex is very strong in newborn babies – some babies even suck their fingers in the womb – it seems to provide a natural comfort fot them. In general, dummies are not harmful to dental development, but it is thought that they may impede linguistic development, limiting a baby's chance to 'babble'.

Recent research has shown that use of a dummy appears to reduce the risk of Sudden Infant Cot Death (SIDS, see page 80) and may also reduce the impact of other known risk factors in the sleep environment. You may find a dummy very helpful in soothing a wakeful and crying baby in the night.

Q Can I spoil my newborn baby by picking him up as soon as he cries?

A No, you will not spoil your baby by picking him up – he needs reassurance and the comfort of knowing you are there. As he gets older and you learn how to interpret his cries, you will come to know more about when he needs your immediate attention.

Q What is 'controlled crying'?

A This is a technique used to settle babies in their cots and teach them how to fall asleep on their own. Basically, you leave your baby to cry, initially for four minutes, and then go in and reassure her, talking to her and stroking her briefly, but never picking her up out of her cot. You repeat the process as many times as necessary, gradually lengthening the time between each visit by a few minutes, until your baby falls asleep on her own. Controlled crying can be distressing and should never be attempted with babies under six months old.

Baby massage

Every baby yearns for loving touch – baby massage is a perfect way to offer this. Gentle massage boosts both your baby's emotional and physical resilience. It acts on muscles and joints to relieve tension, to alleviate any minor, hidden ailments and to promote relaxation. It is not only beneficial for your baby, but also for you, the parent. It can also be used to ease common problems many babies experience.

Find a warm, quiet location, and make sure both you and your baby are in a safe, comfortable position to do the massage. Ideally, your baby should be naked for her massage, but if she seems ill at ease, then start off with her fully clothed. It is best not to massage your baby when she is tired, hungry or full, as this may be uncomfortable for her. Wash your hands in warm water before you start; then loosen them up by rubbing them together and shaking them.

Ease your baby into a massage routine by initially just holding, rocking and stroking

Oils

Use oil when massaging as this prevents friction that might otherwise occur through skin-to-skin contact. Suitable oils are grapeseed, sweet almond, olive oil and organic sunflower oil. Do not use aromatherapy oils as they are too strong for young babies.

her to get the feel of what she likes. It is likely to take a few sessions before your baby gets used to massage, so gently persevere and gradually build your routine. It is only after the age of about two months that you should progress to full body massages. For more details on baby massage techniques, see *Baby Massage* by Peter Walker, also in this series.

SOOTHE IRRITABILITY

Hold your baby close and stroke her gently all over her back and up and down the length of her spine. Talk to her softly as you massage her.

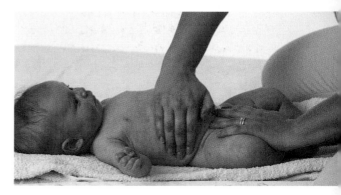

RELIEVE WIND OR COLIC

Using the relaxed weight of your cupped hand, massage your baby's belly in a circular motion from your left to your right. Repeat 4 to 5 times.

COMBAT SLEEPLESSNESS OR ANXIETY

Place your baby in the Tiger in the Tree position by bringing your right hand between her knees and placing your palm flat over her tummy. Tuck her foot into the crook of your arm, turn her over onto your hand, and very gently knead both sides of her tummy with your right hand. Keep massaging for a few minutes. If this does not relax her, try walking around with her in this position.

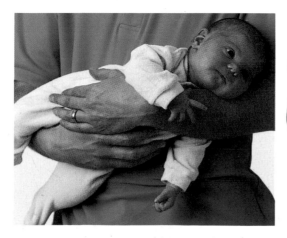

FEEDING YOUR BABY

Whether nursing, bottlefeeding or introducing your baby to first foods, the time that you spend feeding your baby should be special. If you are breastfeeding you'll be able to feed your baby on demand without the need for extra equipment. If you decide to bottle feed, you'll have to learn to make up infant formula and to keep your baby's feeding equipment scrupulously clean. Once weaning starts you will want to make sure that the food you offer is healthy and free from additives, excess salt and sugar.

Breastfeeding

A mother's milk contains all the nutrients her baby needs to thrive for the first six months and it contains antibodies that help to build a strong immune system. Available on demand and at the right temperature, breast milk is also convenient. And the skin-to-skin contact a mother experiences with her child during feeding is unique and fosters mutual love and intimacy.

Your baby's growth during the first six months will be the greatest of her life. At about five months most babies will have doubled their birth weights; by a year they will have roughly tripled them. For physical growth and normal mental development to occur your baby needs to feed regularly.

DEMAND FEEDING

Some mothers worry that their babies are not getting enough milk, or that their breasts are too small and their milk supply is inadequate. Milk is produced in the glands of the breasts, not in the fatty tissue, so breast size has no bearing on milk production. As long as you take your cues from your baby and feed on demand, she should get the nourishment she needs.

Feeding on demand depends entirely on your baby; some babies like to feel full all the time so may require feeding every one to two hours. Others may feed less frequently.

Your breasts are stimulated by your baby to produce the milk she requires, so it is important that you are guided by her appetite and not restricted by a schedule.

1 ENCOURAGE THE ROOTING REFLEX
Position your baby so that she is comfortably cradled in your arms. Stroke your baby's cheek so that she turns towards you, ready to suck.

Benefits of breastfeeding

Breastfed babies suffer less from respiratory illness, gastroenteritis, urinary and ear infections. Breast milk also contains fatty acids that play a vital role in brain development. Breastfeeding is known to reduce the risk of childhood diabetes and allergic conditions such as eczema and is thought to lessen the likelihood of obesity in later life.

Breastfeeding mothers usually regain their shapes more quickly than bottlefeeding mothers because oxytocin, the hormone that stimulates milk production, also makes your uterus contract, and this encourages your abdomen to return to its prebirth size. Breastfeeding can also reduce a woman's risk of breast cancer.

2 OFFER YOUR NIPPLE AND CHECK THAT SHE LATCHES ON PROPERLY
Hold your baby close and turned towards you. Her mouth should be in line with your nipple. Your baby's back should be in a straight line, supported by your arm. Draw her towards you so that she takes the breast deeply into her mouth. To feed successfully, your baby's mouth should cover most of your areola, forming a tight seal. You should feel her tongue pressing your nipple against the palate of her mouth.

3 REMOVE YOUR BREAST
Once you feel your breast is drained of its milk supply, slip your little finger into the side of your baby's mouth to break her suction. Don't pull away before she has released your nipple as this will make your nipple sore.

4 OFFER THE OTHER BREAST
Before you transfer your baby from one side to the other, wind her (see page 36) if necessary. Cradle your baby comfortably in your other arm and offer her your second breast to suckle.

BREASTFEEDING POSITIONS

Although many mothers sit upright on a low chair or with their backs propped up against furniture while nursing, there are times when nursing in bed will be more comfortable or convenient. While your baby is young, experiment with different positions so your baby doesn't insist on latching on in only one. It is a good idea, too, to change positions throughout the day to prevent undue soreness in one part of the breast.

RECLINING POSITION

This is a useful position if you have had an episiotomy and find it painful to sit. It is also good for night feedings. Lie down on your side with plenty of pillows to prop you up and keep you comfortable. Place your baby in the crook of your arm with her mouth in line with your nipple. When she is ready, gently draw her onto your breast.

CLUTCH HOLD

This is a useful position to try if your baby wriggles and arches her back when feeding or if you've had a Caesarean section. Sit upright with your feet close together and your knees up. Put a pillow on your lap and place your baby on her back with her face towards you. Support her head and neck with your hands and use your arm to hold her body close to your side.

Expressing breast milk

There may be times when you cannot be there to breastfeed your child or you would like your partner to give your baby breast milk. To do so, you must express milk beforehand – by hand or with a pump – into a sterile bottle, cup or plastic bag for freezing. After sealing, you should label the container with the date and time of expression. You can store expressed milk in the freezer for up to three months but you must freeze it right away. If it is stored in the refrigerator, be certain to use it within the next 24 hours. Make sure you throw away any unused milk and do not refreeze.

You may also need to express milk if your breasts become engorged, that is, hard and full of milk. Expressing eases the pain and increases the milk flow.

HAND EXPRESSION
Skin-to-skin contact is the best way of stimulating your milk ducts. Make sure your hands are clean and massage your breasts well. Gently stroke down towards the nipple and the areola (the dark area around your nipple), then place your thumbs above the areola and your fingers below. Develop a rhythmic motion of squeezing then pressing back towards your breastbone. After a few minutes, your milk should appear.

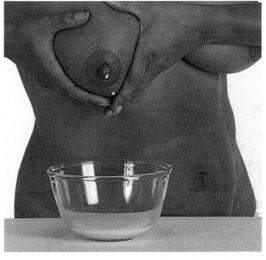

MANUAL PUMP EXPRESSION
A variety of hand pumps are available to make expressing milk faster. The syringe-style pump is the most effective. It has inner and outer cylinders and works by suction, drawing out milk in a piston-type action. Make a tight seal over your nipple with the funnel on the inner cylinder, then draw the outer cylinder in and out in a steady motion for a few minutes until your milk appears.

MACHINE PUMP EXPRESSION
Battery operated machine pumps and small electric ones are available for home use. These pumps express milk quickly by performing the squeezing motion automatically. Machine pumps generally come with a fitting that enables milk to be expressed directly into feeding bottles – making them slightly more convenient to use.

Sterilizing bottles

If you choose to bottlefeed your baby it is important for your baby's health that you maintain a high standard of cleanliness. Milk is the perfect breeding ground for bacteria and if you are not careful your baby could suffer stomach pains and fail to put on weight at a crucial time of his development.

All feeding equipment must be kept scrupulously clean. Bottles, teats, rings and caps must be thoroughly washed individually in warm, soapy water and rinsed clean. The feeding equipment should then be sterilized using chemicals, steam, microwave or a large pan of boiling water. Chemical sterilizing involves using a special sterilizing kit with tablets or a liquid, while steam units are sold for cooker-tops and microwaves. Sterilizing can change the shape of the teats, particularly the hole size, so make sure you check them frequently.

Your young baby will be using up to eight bottles a day, although commercial sterilizers rarely hold more than six; therefore, you will have to plan on doing two loads a day. As your baby gets older, he will need fewer

bottles, which will make your workload easier, but you should still continue to sterilize all feeding equipment for as long as your baby is bottle fed.

TRAVEL TIP
When heading out for the day with your baby, you will have more than enough to think about without having to worry about sterilizing and filling your baby's bottles. Why not make life a little simpler by using bottles of ready-made formula or those with disposable cups? A fuss-free excursion will be a much more enjoyable and relaxing one for both you and your baby.

YOU WILL NEED

bottles, teats, rings, caps

washing-up liquid

bottle brush

special teat-shaped brush

sterilizer, large pan or sterilizer

stacking rack

large paper towels (for draining)

Boiling method

Bottles can be sterilized with boiling water. Submerge and boil for 10 minutes, then let the pan cool while the lid stays on. Use clean hands to remove items on to paper towels and leave to drain.

1 WASH BOTTLES
With warm soapy water, use a bottle brush around the screw thread at the top of the bottle and on the ring where hardened milk can easily get stuck. Rinse thoroughly.

2 WASH TEATS
Clean the surface, then turn the teats inside out and scrub them using a teat brush to ensure that you remove any stubborn milk particles. Rinse thoroughly.

3 FILL THE STERILIZER WITH CHEMICALS
Use the recommended tablets or liquid for your sterilizer and follow the directions on the manufacturer's packaging to make up the concentration or solution.

4 IMMERSE THE EQUIPMENT
Place all feeding equipment into the solution and leave for the recommended time. Drain the sterilizer and rinse the items with cooled boiled water. Use the items immediately or leave them in the sterilizer for up to 24 hours.

Making up formula

Formula milk is usually based on cow's milk and it contains all the vitamins and minerals your baby needs for the first six months. Powdered formula is still the most popular choice, although cartons of ready-made formula are also available. Ready-made formula is more expensive, but the cartons are convenient for the times when you are out and about with your baby.

There are a few basic rules to follow when preparing powdered formula. The most important is to always make sure your hands are clean and that all the equipment you use is sterilized. Follow the manufacturer's measurements to the letter, as they are calculated to suit your baby's needs exactly. Adding too much formula to the water can make your baby ill, while adding too little may result in your baby becoming undernourished.

Although you can make up individual bottles as you need them, you may find it more convenient to make up a day's feeds in one go and store them in the fridge. Always throw away any formula left over from a feed, or made-up formula that has not been consumed, within 24 hours.

A SPECIAL TIME
Whichever method you choose to feed your baby, make it a relaxed time for you both and enjoy the special bonding that takes place.

1 BOIL THE WATER

Fill a kettle with fresh or filtered water and boil. Do not use mineral water or water softened by softeners, as the level of mineral salts in these can be unsuitable for babies. Add the correct amount of cooled, boiled water to each bottle.

2 MEASURE THE FORMULA

Use the scoop provided in the formula tin to measure the required amount. Level off any excess powder with a knife.

3 ADD THE FORMULA AND MIX

Add the recommended number of scoops of formula to each bottle. Screw on the rings and put on the caps. Shake the bottles vigorously so that all the formula ends up well combined with the water. Place the teats in the bottles upside down to keep them clean until ready for use – they should not touch the formula. Store in the fridge.

CAUTION

Measurements

Never heap or pack a scoop of formula or add an extra one, and make sure the amount of water is correct. If the formula is too concentrated, it may make your baby dehydrated; if it's too weak, your baby won't get enough nourishment. To make extra formula, always add more water and powder in the correct proportions.

Bottlefeeding your baby

The two main benefits of bottlefeeding are that you can see how much milk your baby is taking in, and more importantly, that other family members can experience the special bonding that feeding creates.

To recreate the intimacy breastfeeding permits, sit comfortably in a chair or on the sofa with plenty of cushions for support. Keep distractions at bay; try unplugging the phone or having older children occupied in another room. Play some music to help you relax and enjoy the occasion. You may like to bottlefeed topless so your baby can feel and smell your skin while she feeds.

Formula milk takes longer to digest than breast milk so you don't have to feed your baby as frequently as you would if you were breastfeeding. Babies should be fed on demand and most newborns will need feeding every two hours, although this can vary in accordance with your baby's particular needs. After about one month your baby may require feeding every three hours, and by two to three months of age she may only need feeding every four hours. As your baby matures, her sucking ability increases, and she will be able to consume milk at a faster rate. Teats come with different hole sizes so choose one appropriate to your child's age and check the hole size regularly as frequent sterilizing can alter them.

Always start feeding with a fresh bottle of milk each time. Never refrigerate and then reheat a previously warmed bottle.

SPECIAL BABY MILKS

All baby milks marketed in the UK have to contain certain levels of protein, carbohydrate, fats, vitamins and minerals. A special brand may be prescribed if your baby was premature. Vegan mothers can give their babies soya-based infant formula. So, too, can mothers whose babies have an allergic reaction to milk formula or if there is a strong history of allergy in their families. Don't change to non-dairy baby milks without first talking to your doctor or health visitor.

1 CHECK TEMPERATURE
Test the temperature of the milk before giving it to your baby by shaking a few drops onto the inside of your wrist. It should feel warm but not too hot.

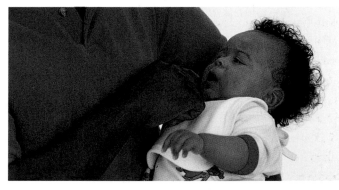

2 ELICIT THE ROOTING REFLEX
If you stroke her cheek, your baby will automatically turn her head towards you with her mouth open, ready to suck.

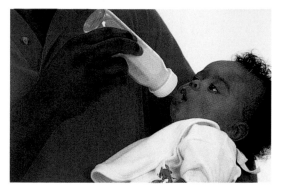

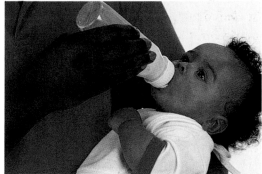

3 INSERT THE TEAT INTO YOUR BABY'S MOUTH
Angle the bottle at about 45 degrees so that the neck of the bottle is full of milk and there are no air bubbles. Place the teat into your baby's mouth.

4 HELP YOUR BABY TO LATCH ON
Make sure the teat does not slip about in your baby's mouth, preventing proper sucking. Hold the bottle steady and adjust the angle of the bottle so that the top is always full of milk.

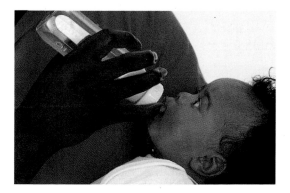

5 REMOVE THE BOTTLE
When your baby has finished, or you want to remove the bottle to wind her, slip your little finger into the side of her mouth to break suction.

Warming milk

Most parents prefer to warm bottled milk to make it more closely resemble breast milk. Most babies, however, don't mind it being cooler as long as the milk is at room temperature, not cold. Do not give a baby milk that has been left to warm for over an hour.

Winding your baby

Whether you breastfeed or bottlefeed your baby, he may take in air along with the milk he ingests. This air can form bubbles in his stomach and may cause discomfort as well as a feeling of fullness. If your baby's stomach hurts, he may cry (see Soothing a crying baby, pages 20–21). If he feels full, he probably won't continue feeding but very soon he will be hungry again. It may help to try and get your baby to expel this accumulated air. Breastfed babies are able to make a tighter seal around their mothers' nipples than bottlefed babies around a bottle's teat, so it is usually sufficient to wind a breastfed baby after he has finished each breast if necessary, while a bottlefed baby may need to be winded more often – after every few ounces. Don't interrupt a feed to wind your baby, however; you should wait until your baby pauses naturally.

BIBS

While being fed, or just after, it is quite common for babies to spit up some milk. It is a good idea, therefore, to protect your baby's clothes with a bib, and your own clothes with a cloth or nappy. A basic towelling bib is all that's required.

ENJOY THIS SPECIAL TIME

Feeding is just as much about emotional nourishment as it is about meeting your baby's nutritional needs. Take this time to relax with your baby, to communicate your love and establish a special rapport.

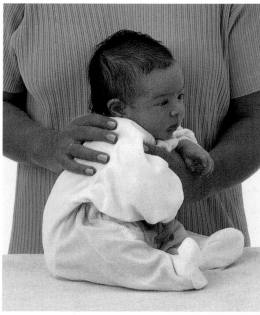

ON YOUR SHOULDER

Lift your baby up so that his head is over your shoulder and facing away from your neck. Use one hand to support his bottom and the other to gently rub or pat his back.

SITTING UP

Gently raise your baby into a sitting position on your lap. Support his head with one hand while you use the other hand to gently rub or pat around his shoulder blades.

Spitting up

It's quite common for a baby to spit up some milk while being winded. This can be as a result of too much swallowed air or too large a meal, or it can be due to the relaxation of the muscles that control the passage between the stomach and the oesophaghus – known medically as reflux. This will happen less and less as your baby grows, so if she is otherwise content, there's nothing to worry about.

ACROSS YOUR KNEES

Lay your baby down so that his tummy rests on one knee and his chest on the other knee or on your crooked arm. His head should face away from you and nothing should obstruct his mouth. Gently rub or pat his back with one or both hands.

Feeding your baby solids

It is recommended that babies should not be given solids until they are around six months old. If you feel your baby is no longer being satisfied by milk alone before this time, ask your health visitor for advice.

Introducing your baby to solids is a big step in her development so start slowly, offering only one food at a time. At first, introduce no more than one or two new tastes every few days. Once your baby is happy with these you can introduce new foods and eventually start mixing different foods together. Don't try to force your baby to eat something she obviously dislikes, wait a week or two and then try again.

Make sure you sterilize your feeding spoon and bowl before use and protect your baby's clothes with a bib. It may take a few weeks for your baby to master the technique of taking the food from the spoon.

Puréeing baby food

At this early stage, all foods must be smoothly puréed to a semi-liquid state – the texture of heavy cream. Use a blender with a sieve, or a 'mouli', which can both liquidize and sieve. Baby (gluten-free) rice mixed with breastmilk or formula is often used as starter food as it has plenty of calories and iron. Other first foods you can offer include puréed vegetables such as sweet potato, broccoli and carrots and fruits such as apple, banana and pear (with no added sugar or salt).

COMMERCIAL BABY FOODS

Although it's best if food is home-made, it can be helpful to have some jars and tins of prepared food on hand when you need them.

- Check the labels to ensure the ingredients are suitable for your baby's age.
- Check the expiry date and that the seals have not been broken.
- Avoid food that contains gluten, nuts, seeds, eggs, fish, citrus fruits and juices, and added sugar.

LET HER EXPERIMENT!
Babies are messy eaters, but using her fingers, your baby is finding out all about the texture of her food as well as its taste, *and* improving her hand-eye coordination. So, although eating with her fingers is messier, she's actually learning valuable lessons.

Beginning solids

At first you will simply want to introduce a couple of spoonfuls of solids halfway through a bottle- or breastfeed. Do not, however, cut down your baby's supply of milk. The puréed food provides only a few extra calories and your baby will still get his essential minerals, vitamins and protein from milk, which should always be given with solids. Over the next few weeks, gradually increase the amount of solids you offer; your baby's need for nourishment from milk will reduce accordingly.

Giving a variety of foods

Try a wide mix of foods but introduce them slowly. Wait a few days after each new food to check for any negative reaction. Your baby will probably prefer blander foods to start with, so avoid strong, spicy tastes.

Spoonfeeding

Hold your baby in an upright position in your lap. Scoop up some of the purée with a long-handled, non-brittle weaning spoon and put it just between her lips so that she can suck the food off. Be careful not to put the spoon too far in her mouth as she may gag. Some of the food will probably reappear until she gets used to taking it off the spoon.

Feeding and weaning

Feeding takes precedence over everything in your baby's first few weeks. Whether you are breast- or bottlefeeding, you should take time to understand the benefits of both methods. Then, suddenly, it's time to start thinking about introducing solid foods – another area of concern. Bear in mind that your baby gives you clues to his or her needs, and if you pay attention to them you won't go far wrong.

Q My doctor said I have inverted or flat nipples. Can I still breastfeed my baby?

A Nipples vary greatly in size and shape, but in all but the most extreme cases, no matter what kind of nipples you have, you will certainly be able to breastfeed your baby. Flat nipples are those that do not to protrude or become erect when stimulated or cold; inverted nipples retract rather than protrude. You may find breast shells worn inside your bra help to draw out flat or inverted nipples.

Q My breasts begin to leak at the most embarrassing moments. Is there anything I can do to prevent this?

A Not all mothers experience leaking, but those who do tend to find it happens especially in the early weeks, while feeding is being established. Nursing pads (disposable and washable, reusable pads) are available to wear in your bra. Changing these pads frequently will help keep your nipples from becoming too moist and possibly sore. Leaking can be minimized by not missing feeds or going longer between feeds than usual. As your body begins to regulate its milk production you will find that this problem goes away.

Q How often should I nurse my baby – and for how long?

A Every baby is different! Healthy, full-term babies may breastfeed as often as every hour or as infrequently as every four hours and still thrive. A baby's breastfeeding patterns can also vary from day to day. Watch for signs of hunger from your baby, such as the rooting reflex (see pages 6–7), chewing or sucking of hands or fingers, or crying. As a guideline, it is recommended that healthy, full-term newborns are breastfed at least eight to 12 times in a 24-hour period, which equates to a feed every two or three hours.

Babies are said to do best when they are breastfed for at least six months.

Q Can I switch between breast- and bottlefeeding?

A Yes, 'mixed' feeding is an option. Most babies can learn to take bottlefeeds between one to three months of age. You can bottlefeed expressed breastmilk or use formula. Breastfed babies may initially be resistant to bottles, so aim to introduce them over at least a couple of weeks so that your baby can get used to the feel of a bottle teat. Start by giving one bottle a day, ideally when your baby is not too hungry and, a few days later, introduce another bottle at another time. Eventually you may be able to alternate bottle and breast.

Q When should I start to wean my baby?

A There is no 'correct' time for weaning all babies, only you can decide what will work best for you and your child. Start when your baby is around six months old, and introduce different foods slowly and patiently. As you wean your child, you can start to cut back on the number of times you breastfeed, but bear in mind that this process may take weeks or months. Some babies are fully weaned within two weeks; others take much longer. Solid foods given at this time primarily give your baby a

chance to become familiar with a variety of tastes and textures.

Q When we start weaning, how much food should I give my baby?

A As a guide, at first one tablespoon of puréed food will be enough, but your baby will soon progress on to two or three spoonsful per meal. After this, use your child's appetite as your guide. From six months your baby will be able to eat chunkier foods. Instead of puréeing food you can begin to mash it, leaving more chunks.

Q When is it safe to give my baby cow's milk?

A Because full-fat milk does not contain the right balance of nutrients to meet your baby's needs, it is not suitable as a drink until your baby is over a year old. Semi-skimmed milk is not suitable for children under two, but you can introduce it from two years old if your child is a good eater and has a varied diet. Skimmed milk is not suitable for children under five.

Helping your baby feed himself

By around six months of age your baby's back and neck muscles may be strong enough to support him sitting unaided in a high chair, which will make feeding easier for both of you. As his hand-mouth coordination improves he will be able to start drinking from a training cup. Once your baby has learned to take food from a spoon he will want to start feeding himself. He'll enjoy gnawing on finger foods when his teeth start to come through, or trying to get food from the bowl into his mouth using his fingers or a spoon. The texture of the food you offer him should become lumpier as he matures.

But self-feeding also means more mess, so be prepared. Use a safe, stable, easy-to-clean high chair with restraints, and spread a mat or newspaper underneath to catch spills. Give your baby a small plastic spoon that won't break and has a limited flicking range, a moulded plastic bib to catch the worst mess,

FROM BOTTLE TO CUP

Trainer cups come in a number of shapes and sizes and sometimes with interchangeable spouts for drinking from. From your baby's viewpoint the critical factor for success is the rate of flow, but this is really a case of trial and error. If the cup you buy first doesn't work for your baby, try a different one – you'll get there in the end.

and shatterproof plastic plates with suction cups on the bottom, which he can't turn over.

The most important thing, though, is to make sure mealtimes are enjoyable. Don't get upset about spills – with your help your baby will soon learn to feed himself happily. Making mealtimes fun will encourage your baby to enjoy himself and promote a healthy attitude towards food in the future.

Success with self-feeding will not only give your baby confidence, but will allow him to join other family members at mealtimes, which will promote his sociability.

FINGER FOODS

Try easy-to-grasp sticks of cooked carrot, pasta, cheese, apple, banana or halved grapes; and small chunks of bread, toast. Avoid giving nuts, fruit with seeds, unpeeled fruit that has a hard skin, and pieces of food that are too small. They may cause your baby to choke.

TRAINER CUPS

Unbreakable plastic feeding cups with weighted bases, tight-fitting lids with integral or changeable spouts, and double handles are recommended when weaning your baby off the bottle. He may prefer to start with water or diluted, unsweetened fruit juice.

EATING WITH HANDS

Don't discourage your baby's attempts to feed himself. If he prefers to use his hands instead of utensils, let him. Ignore any mess; it is important for him to practise feeding himself.

EATING WITH A SPOON

Once your baby's muscles are strong enough, sit her in a high chair but do not leave her unattended. Start off by offering her finger foods or feeding her yourself. She will most likely grab hold of the spoon and attempt to feed herself. A good tip is to load a spoon full of food and swap it for her empty one.

NAPPIES AND NAPPY CHANGING

Your newborn baby will urinate as many as 20 times a day in the first few weeks, so you will spend a lot of your time changing his nappy. When you change your baby make sure you have everything you need by your side – fresh nappy, cotton balls and water, and a nappy sack in which to put the soiled nappy. Being prepared means you don't have to leave your baby alone, wet and exposed. Never leave him unattended on a raised surface; he could easily roll right off. Always clean your baby thoroughly at each changing (see pages 60–61) and make sure your hands are washed afterwards, especially after his polio immunizations as the virus can spread via stool.

Putting on and taking off a disposable nappy

Disposable nappies are currently the most popular choice for parents because they are convenient and easy to use. You don't have to wash them or worry about pins, liners or plastic pants. However, they are expensive – particularly if you plan on having more children – and many people worry about their effect on the environment. Make sure the nappy fits snugly around your baby's thighs. Adjust the waist so that you can fit one finger between your baby's tummy and the nappy.

GET DAD INVOLVED
Nappy changing is the perfect job to help nervous new fathers feel more fully involved in parenting.

Watch out!

A baby boy may be stimulated to urinate by the feel of air on his skin, so keep a spare nappy handy to cover his penis, just in case.

PUTTING ON A DISPOSABLE NAPPY

1 OPEN OUT THE NAPPY AND PLACE UNDER YOUR BABY'S BOTTOM
Lay your baby on his back on a changing mat or other flat surface. Lift his legs up by the ankles and slide an opened nappy under his bottom.

2 BRING THE FRONT UP BETWEEN HIS LEGS
Gently let go of his ankles and bring the front of the nappy up between his legs. For a boy, make sure his penis points downwards so he doesn't urinate into the waistband.

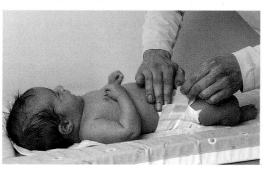

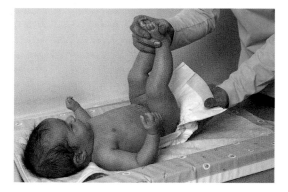

3 FASTEN THE SIDES
Smooth the nappy over his tummy. Bring one side into the middle, unpeel the protective backing to the tab and stick down. Repeat the process with the other side. Fold the top of the nappy in neatly against his tummy.

TAKING OFF A DISPOSABLE NAPPY

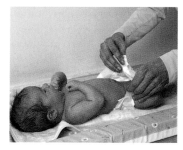

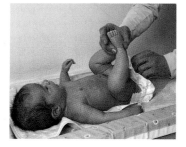

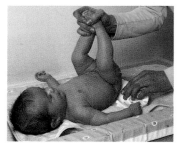

1 FIRST UNFASTEN THE SIDES
Unpeel the tab from one side of the nappy, then the other. Take the front down between your baby's legs.

2 USE THE NAPPY TO CLEAN ANY MESS
Use the front of the nappy to wipe your baby's bottom clean of any excrement.

3 ROLL UP AND REMOVE
Fold the sides in towards the middle, roll the nappy up and slide it from under your baby's bottom. Retape the rolled-up bundle and put it in a nappy sack.

Putting on and taking off a fabric nappy

Fabric nappies can be folded in a variety of ways to suit the shape and size of your baby (see Other types of nappy fold, page 48). A popular nappy fold for a young baby is the rectangle fold (see below). Pre-shaped fabric nappies are also available (see page 49).

In certain circumstances, a properly folded fabric nappy will better contain urine and excrement than a disposable. A fabric nappy also allows more air to circulate around your baby's bottom so the chances of skin irritation and nappy rash are reduced.

Fabric nappies are made of 100 per cent cotton so are not waterproof by themselves; you will need to use some plastic pants on top. Terrycloth nappies are the most absorbent but also the bulkiest. Flatter weave versions are also available. Fabric nappies and plastic pants will make your baby's bottom a few sizes bigger, so keep this in mind when you are shopping for clothes for your baby.

One-way nappy liners that draw urine away from the skin will help keep your baby's skin drier and prevent excrement soiling the nappy.

YOU WILL NEED

fine muslin squares for a newborn

standard square fabric or shaped fabric nappies for an older baby

nappy liners (optional)

nappy pins with safety heads

plastic pants with popper fasteners

PUTTING ON A FABRIC NAPPY

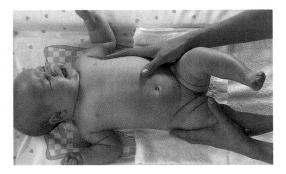

1 PLACE YOUR BABY ON THE NAPPY
Fold the fabric square in half to form a rectangle. Fold the short side of the rectangle a third of the way into the middle. If you are putting a nappy on a girl, place the extra thickness under her bottom. For a boy, position the extra thickness at the front to give more protection over his penis. Lower your baby on to the nappy, aligning her waist with the top.

2 BRING THE FABRIC UP BETWEEN YOUR BABY'S LEGS
Gather the corners of the fabric in your hands and pull it up between her legs, smoothing the front over her stomach.

3 PIN THE SIDES AND PUT ON THE PANTS
Keeping your hand between the fabric and
your baby's skin, pin one side. Adjust the fit, then
fasten another pin on the other side. Slip the
open plastic pants under your baby's bottom and
take the front of the pants up between her legs.
Making sure the nappy is well tucked inside the
plastic pants, fasten one side of the poppers and
then the other.

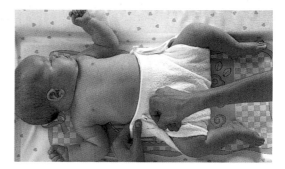

TAKING OFF A FABRIC NAPPY

Most babies do not enjoy having their
bottoms exposed to the air, and may react
negatively to having their nappies taken off.
Make sure you have everything you need – a
clean nappy, cotton balls and water and fresh
clothes, if necessary – close by.

To give your baby's bottom a chance to air
and help prevent nappy rash, incorporate play
into your nappy-changing sessions. Tickle
her, kiss her skin, and generally communicate
with your baby. This will make changing time
fun rather than just a mundane task.

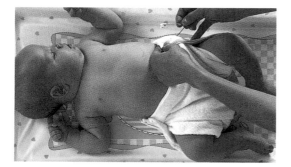

1 UNFASTEN THE NAPPY
Lay your baby on a changing mat. If using
pins, place your hand between the fabric and
her skin and carefully unfasten
each one. Place the pins
out of your baby's reach.
With pre-shaped nappies,
simply pull back the fabric
on each side.

2 LOWER THE FRONT OF THE NAPPY
BETWEEN YOUR BABY'S LEGS
Slowly lower the nappy to check the
damage. If there is any mess, hold
your baby's ankles with one hand,
raising her bottom, and use the
front edge of the fabric to wipe
away any excrement.

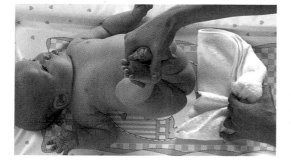

3 ROLL UP AND REMOVE THE NAPPY
FROM UNDERNEATH
With your baby's bottom still raised, fold the sides
of the nappy into the middle and slide the nappy
out from underneath her bottom, rolling it up as
you remove it.

OTHER TYPES OF FABRIC NAPPY FOLD

In addition to the rectangle fold (see Putting on a fabric nappy, page 46), there are a number of other ways to fold fabric nappies to suit your baby's particular shape and needs. The triangle fold is the simplest and requires one pin only. The kite fold produces a neater shape, is very absorbent and is suitable for a growing baby; it needs two pins. You can adjust the size by varying the depth of the last fold (see below).

TRIANGLE FOLD

On a changing mat or other surface, take two diagonally opposite corners of the square fabric and fold into a triangle. Place your baby on top of the nappy, making sure her waist is aligned with the top of the long edge of the triangle. Take one corner of the triangle into the middle, wrapping it well around your baby's tummy. Repeat with the other side. Finish by taking the remaining point of the triangle up between your baby's legs and fasten all three layers with a large nappy pin.

KITE FOLD

1 BRING TWO SIDES INTO THE CENTRE
Place the nappy in front of you. Bring two adjoining sides into the centre to produce a kite shape.

2 FOLD TOP POINT INTO THE CENTRE
Take the point at the top of the kite and neatly fold it down into the middle.

3 FOLD BOTTOM POINT INTO THE CENTRE
You can adjust the depth of this fold to make the surface area larger. Align the top edge with your baby's waist and bring the shorter edge between her legs. Pin each side.

Putting on a pre-shaped nappy

These nappies come already tailored to fit a baby's bottom, so you don't have to fold them or fiddle about with nappy pins. Most have elasticated legs and waist, as well as self-stick tabs or snap fastenings. Pre-shaped nappies usually have a separate waterproof cover. You may also want to use a nappy liner.

All-in-one nappies are pre-shaped and act like regular disposables. They come with an inner absorbent layer, self-stick tabs or snap fastenings, elasticated legs and a waterproof cover.

Both types wash and wear like ordinary fabric nappies, although you should check the care label before soaking them in sterilizing solution as some brands may affect the elastic around the legs and waist.

1 PLACE BABY ON TOP OF THE OPEN NAPPY
Open up the nappy and place on a changing mat. Put your baby on the nappy, aligning her waist with the top.

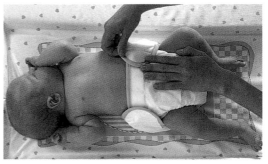

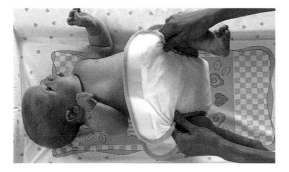

2 BRING THE FRONT OF THE NAPPY UP BETWEEN HER LEGS
Pull the front of the nappy taut and bring it up between your baby's legs. It should fit snugly, but not too tightly, around your baby's thighs.

3 FASTEN THE SIDES
Bring one side over and fasten it with the self-stick tab or snap fastening. Repeat on the other side. If the nappy is not fitting her tummy snugly enough, undo and refasten the sides.

Caring for soiled fabric nappies

While re-usable fabric nappies have many advantages, sterilizing, washing and drying them is a laborious process. To minimize the fuss, make sure that you are well organized beforehand (see box). Incomplete cleaning can leave waste ammonia or bacteria on the nappy that can lead to nappy rash and infection. Using too much detergent on nappies, however, will irritate your baby's sensitive skin. Therefore, measure the amount of cleaner carefully and rinse everything twice.

To thoroughly sterilize nappies leave them to soak for at least six hours in a bucketful of sterilizing solution. Remember to use different buckets for soiled and urine-soaked nappies. A different colour for each bucket will help you tell them apart. The buckets should be big enough to hold at least six nappies but should not be too heavy to pick up when filled with water. Make sure they have sturdy handles and tightly fitting lids.

With soiled nappies, scrape as much excrement into the toilet bowl as possible, then rinse them. If you are using biodegrad-able nappy liners simply remove the liner with the stool and flush down the toilet. Then place the soiled nappy to soak in the bucket with the lid tightly sealed.

Rinse urine-soaked nappies under a tap then wring out the moisture. Wash plastic pants with some washing-up liquid in water that is neither too hot nor too cold, otherwise they will go hard. If they do stiffen, soften them by tumble drying on a low setting for 10 minutes.

You may prefer to use a nappy laundry service. The dirty nappies are collected twice a week and a supply of clean, fresh nappies is delivered to your door. Although a more expensive option, you may find it convenient.

1 FILL TWO BUCKETS WITH
STERILIZING SOLUTION
Always wear gloves when handling sterilizing solution and keep it out of the reach of older children.

2 PUT NAPPIES INTO BUCKETS
Rinse urine-soaked nappies under a tap then wring them out. Scrape off or flush excrement from soiled nappies into the toilet bowl. Submerge urine-soaked nappies in one bucket and soiled nappies in another. Leave to soak for at least six hours.

3 USE TONGS TO REMOVE NAPPIES
Wring out nappies thoroughly and dispose of solution carefully. Rinse urine-soaked nappies in hot water and leave to dry. Wash soiled nappies on the hot cycle of your washing machine and rinse them twice.

4 WASH PLASTIC PANTS
Add some washing-up liquid to a bowl of warm water. Wash plastic pants in the bowl then take them out and leave to dry. If they become stiff you can soften them by tumble drying on a low setting.

DRESSING YOUR BABY

Young babies generally don't like being dressed or undressed as they dislike the feeling of air on their skin and garments being placed over their heads. Make it easier on your baby and yourself by having everything within reach. Never leave your baby alone on a raised surface – whether or not he can turn over.

Make dressing fun with lots of nuzzling and kissing, but take extra care to be gentle. The clothes that you choose should reflect this sensitivity. Natural fabrics like cotton and wool will be warm and also allow your baby's skin to breathe, but avoid scratchy material – remember how much you hated itchy clothes when you were a child? Always wash your baby's clothes before first use with a non-biological powder.

Putting on and taking off a vest

Your baby's ability to regulate his own body temperature is not fully functional for the first few months of his life. As a result, he can very easily become too hot or too cold. Unless it is very warm, always dress your baby in a vest. In very hot weather he may wear just a vest and nappy.

Dress and undress your baby somewhere warm, and be ready either to dress him again quickly, or to wrap him up in a warm towel or blanket. Comfort your baby by nuzzling his tummy. Skin-to-skin contact is very important in promoting a loving relationship, and dressing and undressing give caregivers excellent opportunities to foster this intimacy.

Vest designs vary, but they all account for the disproportionately large size of a baby's head. Their wide, loose necks will prevent your baby from becoming distressed by having material dragged over his face.

PUTTING ON A VEST

1 PLACE THE VEST BEHIND HIS HEAD
Using both hands, gather the material to the neck and stretch the opening wide. Gently raise his head and slip the vest over his head and neck.

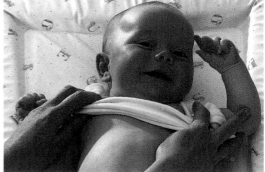

2 ADJUST FABRIC AND LOCATE SLEEVE
Straighten the fabric around his neck. Take hold of one sleeve, gather up the material and insert your hand.

4 STRAIGHTEN THE VEST
Gently smooth the fabric down over his back and front and, if applicable, fasten the poppers between his legs. Take care not to pinch his skin.

3 PULL THE SLEEVE GENTLY OVER YOUR BABY'S ARM
Keeping hold of your baby's wrist, gently ease the sleeve over his arm with your free hand. Repeat with the other sleeve.

TAKING OFF A VEST

To take the vest off, begin by freeing your baby's arms. Slip the vest over the front, then the back, of your baby's head. Make a game of bending down close and kissing his tummy as you lift off the vest – he may never notice it's gone! As before, avoid dragging the material over your baby's face.

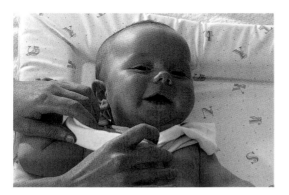

1 GENTLY EASE YOUR BABY'S ARM OUT
Gather the sleeve up in one hand and use your other hand to gently guide your baby's arm out of the sleeve. Repeat on the other side.

2 BRING THE VEST UP TO HIS NECK
Concertina the material at your baby's neck. Use both hands to stretch the opening of the neck as wide as possible.

3 LIFT UP AND REMOVE THE VEST
Being careful to not touch his face with the material, pull the vest up over his face to the crown of his head in one smooth motion. Then gently lift his head and take the vest away.

Your baby's wardrobe

Buying clothes for your baby is great fun, but try to resist buying too many clothes before the big day, because if yours is a big baby, the 'newborn' size may not fit her for long! If your baby's weight is projected to be 4.5 kg (10 lbs) or more, you may want to start with a three-month size.

Choose clothes that are easy to put on and take off, avoid anything that needs handwashing or ironing, check all items for raised seams and scratchy labels and choose natural fibres that 'breathe' as these minimize irritation and sweating.

The basic layette

ALL-IN-ONE SUITS

Also known as babygrows, these suits, with poppers up the front and around the crotch, are the most practical items for day- and nightwear. They give easy access for nappy changing and keep baby warm – but not too warm. Make sure that there is always plenty of growing room in the legs and feet, as your young baby's bones are soft and a tight suit may hamper her growth.

VESTS

These should have wide or envelope necks so that they can be slipped easily over the baby's head. Many vests also fasten under the crotch with poppers, providing extra warmth and keeping the nappy securely in place. Once again, keep clothing loose so that your baby can grow into it.

NIGHTWEAR

Most baby nightdresses have drawstring bottoms to keep baby's feet warm. If not, you will need socks. You may prefer to dress your baby in an all-in-one sleep suit or, if it's warm, put her down to sleep in a vest and nappy.

OUTDOOR CLOTHES

Babies lose a great deal of heat from their bare heads, which are proportionately large for their bodies, so a hat is essential in winter and may be advisable in spring and autumn.

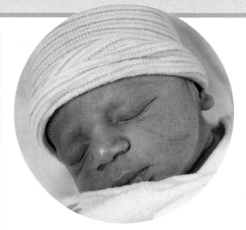

IF YOU WANT TO GET AHEAD, GET A HAT

A simple cotton hat can be invaluable in the early days, keeping your baby warm or protecting her from too much sun.

A sun hat is essential for summer if you plan to spend a lot of time outdoors in the sunshine. If it's very cold and your pushchair doesn't provide much protection from the elements, you will need a baby nest. Shawls, cardigans and mittens are all useful for the cold and should be close-knitted to prevent tiny fingers getting trapped. If it gets very hot, invest in a few lightweight summer romper suits.

THE RIGHT CHOICE

Clothes can become dirty or stained very quickly, particularly in the nappy area and neckline, so they will need to be changed and washed frequently. Buy colourfast, machine-washable clothes that are suitable for tumble-drying. Avoid synthetic fabrics that can be scratchy against newborn skin, and choose natural fabrics such as cotton and wool instead.

ALL-IN-ONE STRETCH SUITS

Short-sleeved cotton jumpsuits with poppers at the crotch don't ride up like bottomless vests and keep your baby warmer. The envelope neck makes them easy to put over your baby's head, and the poppers allow you access when you want to change her nappy. Long-sleeved babygrows with poppers around the legs and crotch are great for young babies. Warm and easy to wear, they don't restrict your baby's movement. Make sure there's always plenty of growing room in the legs.

Putting on and taking off a jumpsuit

An all-in-one jumpsuit is a staple of most babies' wardrobes. It is easy to put on and take off, and covers the whole body, including the feet, so that you don't need to bother with booties.

When buying a jumpsuit, choose one that is colourfast and soft – natural fibres are always best. When selecting the size, use your baby's height and weight as a guide, rather than age, since babies vary widely in their rates of growth.

If you have a choice, go for looser, baggier jumpsuits that will give your baby a bit of growing space. Pay particular attention to the neck, which, when the poppers are fastened, should be loose and should not constrict your baby's movement in any way.

PUTTING ON A JUMPSUIT

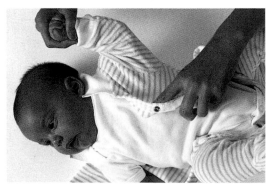

1 PUT THE FEET AND LEGS ON
Open out the jumpsuit on a non-slip surface and lay your baby on top of it. Gather up the material of one leg and slide it over his foot, making sure his toes go all the way in. Carry the material up his leg. Repeat for the other foot.

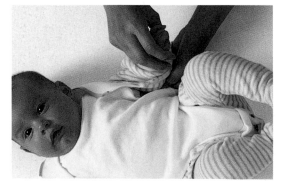

2 PUT ONE SLEEVE ON
Gather up the sleeve material and gently slide it over your baby's wrist, making certain that his fingers and nails don't get caught in the fabric.

3 COVER HIS ARM AND SHOULDER
Slide the material down his arm and over his shoulder. Pull on the material rather than his arm. Now put on the other sleeve. If the sleeves are too long, fold back the cuffs so his hands are free.

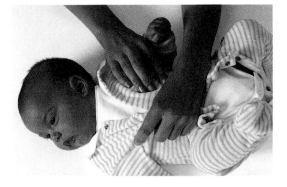

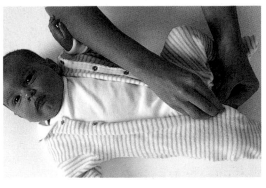

4 STRAIGHTEN THE TWO SIDES
Adjust the jumpsuit so the two sides meet in the centre. Align the poppers.

5 FASTEN THE POPPERS
Starting at his crotch and working up, do up the poppers. Make sure you join the crotch poppers correctly as it's easy to make a mistake.

TAKING OFF A JUMPSUIT

Your baby may need a change of clothes as often as a change of nappy. Jumpsuits make changing easy: they are easy to undo and take off, and you can change your baby in stages so that he doesn't get upset by being completely undressed. If you are only changing his nappy, leave the top of his jumpsuit on while you attend to his bottom. If a full change of clothing is needed, attend to his bottom, then slip a clean jumpsuit on to his bottom half before removing the top half of the dirty suit.

1 REMOVE THE FABRIC FROM HIS LEGS
Undo all the poppers. Support his knee while you gently ease the material away from his leg. Repeat on the other side.

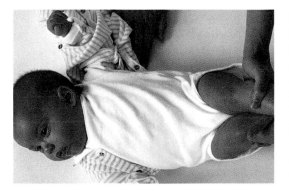

2 SLIDE THE SUIT UP HIS BACK
If you're going to remove the suit, lift your baby's legs while you gently push it up under his back to his shoulders.

3 REMOVE THE SLEEVES FROM HIS ARMS
Hold your baby's elbow while you gather up the sleeve and gently ease it away from his wrist. Repeat for the other arm.

KEEPING YOUR BABY CLEAN

Your newborn will probably object to being immersed in water, so you may want to delay giving her a full bath until she is a bit older. A newborn has very sensitive skin and a limited potential for getting dirty, so you can keep her clean by wiping her down with water and cotton wool. Some doctors recommend that babies shouldn't be immersed in water until their umbilical cord stumps have fallen off and any circumcisions have healed.

Once you feel confident about giving your baby a bath, you'll find it easier to wash her in a baby bath. When your baby can sit up unaided you can start using the proper bath. By this stage your baby will probably look upon bathtime as one of the highlights of her day. Always use specially formulated baby toiletries on your baby's delicate skin.

When you do bathe her, do so as quickly as possible, making sure that the room is warm and that you have a soft, fluffy towel ready to wrap her in as soon as you've finished. The key is to be prepared – have everything you need at hand because you must never leave your baby unattended in the bath.

Cleaning a newborn

A simple once-over is all your young baby needs, since only her exposed areas – face, neck creases, hands, feet – and genitals and bottom are likely to become dirty. (See pages 60–61 for advice on cleaning your baby's bottom and page 72 for advice on cleaning the umbilical cord area.)

To clean your newborn use cotton wool – a clean pad for every pass – and cooled boiled water. Do not use tap water at this stage as you will be cleaning your baby's eyes, or talcum powder or soap as they will dry her very sensitive skin. Equally, avoid cleaning inside your baby's nose or ears; your baby's inner surfaces are lined with mucous membranes that clean themselves – interfering with them will do more harm than good. Your newborn's limbs may still be curled up against her body, so you may need to gently ease them apart.

YOU WILL NEED

bowl of cooled boiled water – once your baby is older you can simply use warm water from the tap

plenty of cotton wool

plastic bag for disposing of dirty cotton wool

flannel for any accidental spillages

towel

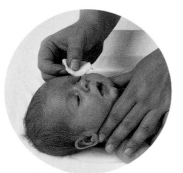

1 CLEAN AROUND YOUR BABY'S EYES

Using cooled boiled water, wet some cotton wool and wipe from the inner to the outer corner of her eye. Use fresh cotton wool for the other eye to prevent transferring infections. Use more cotton wool to wipe around and behind the ears, but not inside.

2 OPEN OUT HER HANDS

Use some more cotton wool to wipe her hands, unclenching them to check for sharp fingernails and dirt between the fingers. Pat dry with a soft towel or cloth.

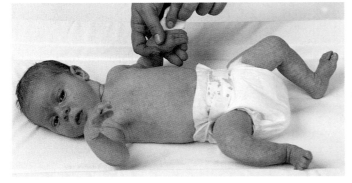

3 CLEAN YOUR BABY'S FEET

Wipe the top and bottom of your baby's feet, and between her toes. They may be tightly curled so gently ease them apart. Again, pat dry with a towel.

4 TUMMY AND LEGS

Holding your baby firmly but gently, moisten some cotton wool and wipe her tummy area. Using fresh cotton wool clean along the folds of your baby's legs. Wipe downwards and away from her body to avoid transmitting any infections to her genital area.

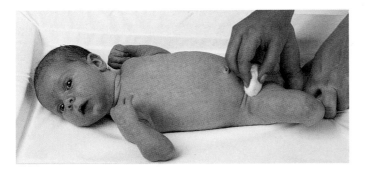

Cleaning your baby's bottom

When you change your baby's nappy, clean his or her bottom thoroughly. It is a good idea to expose this area to the air for a while to give the skin a rest from being covered. The basic methods of cleaning this area are, of course, the same, but there are a few things to bear in mind depending on whether you are cleaning a boy or a girl.

BOWEL MOVEMENTS AND MECONIUM

The first stools your newborn produces will be dark in colour and sticky in texture. This is meconium – the substance which lined your baby's intestines while he or she was in the uterus. After meconium is passed, bowel movements will become paler and firmer.

TIPS FOR CLEANING A BOY

Your baby boy may urinate when you remove his nappy, so do so slowly. His urine can spray widely, so wipe down his abdomen and legs, or the urine can remain on his skin and cause irritation.

Using fresh cotton wool, wipe his penis using a downward motion – don't pull his foreskin back. Clean around his testicles as well. Holding your baby's ankles, lift his bottom gently and clean around his anal area and the backs of his thighs. Pat the whole area thoroughly dry.

If your baby boy has been circumcised you may need to apply a new dressing over the wound when you change his nappy for the first day or two. Use a light dressing such as gauze and put petroleum jelly on the gauze so that it won't stick to his skin.

A circumcised penis will probably take seven to 10 days to heal, during which time the tip of the penis may be red and raw. Watch out for any signs of infection. If there is persistent bleeding, fever, pus-filled blisters or swelling, consult your baby's doctor.

TIPS FOR CLEANING A GIRL

When cleaning a girl, hold her ankles gently with one hand, put your finger between her ankles, and lift her bottom slightly. Using fresh cotton wool, clean the outer lips of her vulva – but don't clean inside. This area is not likely to be dirty and if you open up the folds you may introduce unnecessary infection. Always wipe from front to back so as not to spread any bacteria from the anus to the vagina, and use fresh cotton wool for each swipe. Keeping her bottom raised, clean her buttocks and the backs of her thighs and dry the whole area thoroughly.

You may also notice some slight bleeding or a white discharge coming from your newborn's vagina. Usually this is due to maternal hormones still circulating inside her body. It is quite normal and should cease after a few days.

YOU WILL NEED

bowl of cooled boiled water – once your baby is older you can simply use warm water from the tap

plenty of cotton wool

plastic bag for disposing of dirty cotton wool and soiled nappy

clean nappy

flannel for any accidental spillages

towel

1 USE THE NAPPY TO CLEAN YOUR BABY'S BOTTOM

If your baby has had a bowel movement, use the edge of the nappy to clean some of the mess from her bottom.

2 CLEAN YOUR BABY'S TUMMY

Hold your baby firmly but gently on the changing mat. The tightly curled limbs of a newborn may need to be gently eased away from her torso. Moisten clean cotton wool in some cooled boiled water and use to wipe all over her tummy area. After the umbilical cord area has healed, you can use plain water.

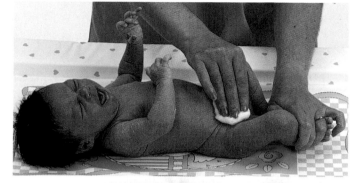

3 WIPE INTO YOUR BABY'S LEG CREASES

Taking fresh cotton wool, clean into the folds of your baby's legs. Wipe gently downwards and away from her body.

4 CLEAN YOUR BABY'S GENITALS

Hold your baby's ankles with one hand and gently lift. Use fresh, moist cotton wool to clean the outer lips of your baby's genital area. Do not open out the lips to clean inside. Use fresh cotton wool for each swipe and always wipe downwards, so that you don't transfer any bacteria from the anus to the vagina.

5 CLEAN YOUR BABY'S BUTTOCKS

Still keeping your baby's bottom raised from the changing mat, take fresh moistened cotton wool and wipe her anal area clean. Make sure you also clean the backs of her thighs and up her back, if necessary.

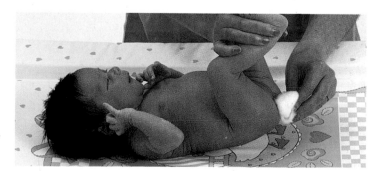

Common skin conditions

As soft and glowing as your newborn's skin may seem, it is also very delicate, and very few babies have completely flawless skin during their first months of life. In the first few weeks after leaving the uterus, maternal hormones continue to circulate through your newborn's system, stimulating the sebaceous glands and making your baby susceptible to conditions such as infantile acne and cradle cap. Also, because the skin's defence systems have not fully matured, your newborn's sensitive skin is particularly vulnerable to the effects of temperature, microbial infection and irritants, and skin conditions such as nappy rash and miliaria are common. Most of these conditions are harmless and will usually clear as your baby grows older.

Spots and rashes

INFANTILE ACNE

A few weeks after birth, some babies develop acne-type lesions on the face, thought to occur as a result of maternal hormones still present in the baby's bloodstream. These hormones cause an overproduction of oily sebum – in the same way that hormonal changes at puberty can result in teenage spots. The acne will usually clear spontaneously, but if the pimples become infected they may need treatment from a doctor.

ERYTHEMA TOXICUM

This harmless rash affects many babies in the early days of life. The rash may consist of tiny, firm yellow or white bumps, sometimes filled with fluid, surrounded by a ring of redness. This fluid may look like pus, but is only blood cells and is not infectious. It may also present as red splotches instead of bumps. The rash may appear on your baby's face or trunk or it may cover the whole body. There is no treatment as such, but the rash will disappear within a few days.

MILIA

Often referred to as 'milk spots', milia are tiny white or yellow pimples that are caused by a blockage of the sebaceous glands by keratin from old skin cells or oily sebum. Milia are harmless, and usually disappear quickly without treatment, although they can sometimes persist for up to two to three months.

MILIARIA

Also known as prickly heat or heat rash, the many, tiny spots and blisters of miliaria develop when excessive and sudden sweating causes a blockage of your baby's sweat glands. The rash tends to occur around areas of skin prone to sweating and can be very uncomfortable. Young babies are particularly susceptible to miliaria. To prevent it, be careful not to allow your baby to overheat, and avoid overdressing him. Calamine lotion and frequent cool baths can help to relieve the discomfort. The rash should disappear soon after your baby has cooled down, but the sweat glands may remain blocked for several weeks.

CRADLE CAP

SIGNS OF CRADLE CAP

Some babies' skins produce an excess of oil, resulting in yellow, scaly patches that look like a bad case of dandruff. This can irritate the skin, leading to redness, particularly on the scalp.

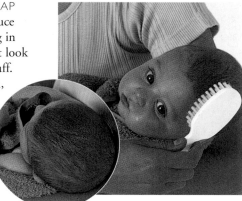

TREATING CRADLE CAP

You can soften the scales by massaging baby oil into the scalp. Leave overnight then brush the scales off the next morning with a soft brush. You may need to repeat the treatment several times.

NAPPY RASH

Too little contact with sun and air, and frequent exposure to excess moisture and the chemicals found in urine and faeces can lead the skin to become red and inflamed. This can develop into nappy rash. Although rarely serious, nappy rash can be uncomfortable and distressing for your baby, and it left untreated it could become infected. To prevent this, make sure you change your baby's nappy more regularly, thoroughly cleaning the whole nappy area with plain water every time and drying thoroughly.

AIR IS BENEFICIAL

Expose your baby's bottom to air and sunshine by letting her go without a nappy for short periods frequently throughout the day. Just after a nappy change is a good time.

SIGNS OF NAPPY RASH

A red rash, or raised spots around the bottom or in the fatty folds between your baby's legs are sure signs.

TREATING NAPPY RASH

Your health visitor or pharmacist may suggest a nappy rash cream. Seek advice if the rash persists or worsens – it may be thrush.

Giving your baby a sponge bath

Doctors and midwives generally recommend that babies are given sponge baths until the umbilical stump has fallen off and the area has fully healed. But some older babies also get upset at the prospect of being immersed in a bath (and a parent may find the idea of trying to hold a slippery, squirming baby quite daunting, too) so a sponge bath can be a good alternative.

Once your baby can hold his head up, you can sit him in your lap and clean him one bit at a time. As your baby may dislike being undressed and being wet, a sponge bath avoids both these problems.

Make sure everything you need is at hand: bowls of warm water – one with baby wash, the other for rinsing – and a sponge or soft flannel. Spread a large fluffy towel over your lap. You might want to wear an apron to keep yourself dry; terrycloth with a waterproof backing will be softer against your baby's skin than plastic.

Undress your baby a little bit at a time, and wrap him up in the towel to keep him warm, redressing him as you finish bathing and drying each area. Use a wrung-out sponge to prevent water dripping on your baby.

Sponge washing the hair

If you are worried about washing your baby's hair, or if he resists proper shampooing, you don't have to undress him or put him in a bath. Simply sit him on your lap as for a sponge bath and wash his hair and head with a damp sponge or flannel. Pat dry with a soft towel and gently brush his hair.

LITTLE BY LITTLE
If your baby gets upset or won't stay still long enough for a complete sponge bath, why not do it step by step at intervals throughout the day? Each time you change his nappy, for example, you could sponge-bathe another area.

1 WIPE YOUR BABY'S FACE

Before undressing your baby, wet the cloth with clean water and wipe his face, paying particular attention to the eye and mouth areas. Pat dry, if necessary.

2 WASH HIS CHEST

Take off your baby's top. Wet the cloth with soapy water and clean his chest, making sure to clean in his skin folds and under the arms. Do not scrub. Rinse off the soap with clean water.

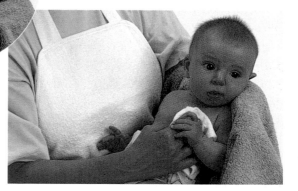

3 PAT HIS CHEST DRY WITH THE TOWEL

Pick up the end of the towel and use it to remove any water by pressing lightly.

4 THEN WASH HIS BACK

Supporting him with your arm, lean your baby forward, then wash, rinse and dry his back. Put his top back on.

5 NOW ATTEND TO HIS LEGS

Remove his nappy, and with the damp, soapy cloth, clean your baby's legs, paying particular attention to his thigh creases and the skin behind the knees. Rinse and pat dry.

6 FINALLY, WASH HIS HANDS AND FEET

Clean his hands and between the fingers, then wipe the top and bottom of his feet, and between the toes. Then pat dry.

Preparing to bathe your baby

Before you start bathing your baby, have everything you need at hand. The first rule of bathing is 'never leave your baby unattended in the bath'. By being well prepared you won't have to go looking for things holding a wet baby.

WASHING YOUR BABY'S HAIR

You will need to wash your baby's hair and scalp with warm water every couple of days during the first few weeks to remove any sweat and dirt. There is no need for shampoo until your baby's hair has grown, then a gentle baby shampoo can be used.

Your baby may object quite strongly to having her head wet. Babies especially dislike getting water on their faces or in their eyes, so you should take care to avoid this. If your baby really hates having her hair washed, don't force her to endure the procedure. Instead, simply wipe her head clean with a sponge or soft face cloth for a couple of weeks, then try again. Remember: your baby will not be happy if she feels insecure, so if she objects to being held under your arm, sit

Test the water

Your baby has sensitive skin. The bath water should be pleasantly warm but not hot. Test the temperature with your elbow, but if you are not sure, use a bath thermometer. It should read 30°C (85°F). When using the big bath, try to keep your baby away from the taps – he could scald himself on the hot tap. In fact it's best to run a little cold water into the bath last of all so that if he does touch the tap he won't be burned.

on the edge of the bath and hold her in your lap. Gently pat your baby's head dry.

Cradle cap is common on a baby's scalp (see common skin conditions, pages 62–3). It is no cause for concern and usually clears up after a few weeks.

PREPARING THE BATH

While you are using a portable bath to bathe your baby you can wash her in any room. Make sure the room is sufficiently warm, and the bath is well supported on a waterproof surface away from any draughts.

Fill the bath with only 5–8 cms (2–3 ins) of water for babies up to six months old and never more than waist high (in a sitting position) for older babies. Always put cold water in first and then add hot water to make sure there is no risk of your baby being scalded, but add a little cold water at the end to ensure the taps are cooled.

YOU WILL NEED

baby bath with a textured non-slip base

waterproof apron with plastic backing

mild baby toiletries

small bowl of cooled boiled water

cotton wool

large, soft towels

sponge or soft flannel

clean nappy and clothes

1 CLEAN YOUR BABY'S FACE
Using clean cotton wool and cooled boiled water for a young baby, clean around her eyes and mouth. For an older baby you can use a washcloth and plain water.

2 WASH YOUR BABY'S HAIR
With your baby tucked under your arm, check the water temperature and, using your free hand, take some of the water over her head onto her hair. Gently apply some specially formulated baby shampoo, then rinse it off.

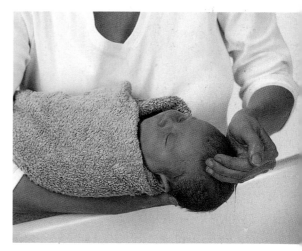

3 TOWEL-DRY YOUR BABY'S HAIR
Gently pat, rather than rub, your baby's hair dry with a towel. Use a corner of the towel as covering her face with it may frighten her. Gently brush her hair with a soft-bristled brush.

Hair shield
To prevent any shampoo or soapy water getting in an older baby's eyes, you could try a hair shield, which fits around the hairline and catches any drips.

Bathing your baby

Until your baby can sit up unsupported – at around six months of age – bathe him in a small plastic bath set at about waist height to avoid hurting your back. If you use a bath stand, make sure it is very stable. A rubber mat in the bottom of the bath will make it less slippery and give your baby more grip, but support his back and shoulders with one hand the entire time he is in the bath. Above all, *never* leave your baby unattended.

Help your baby enjoy his bath by smiling and talking to him throughout; be gentle and avoid getting water on his face. Take care to ensure that the bath water remains warm.

In general, wash the cleanest parts of your baby first and the dirtiest parts last. This way you cut down on the risk of transferring germs from one part of his body to another.

Baby bath float

A baby bath float can be used in the big bath to keep your baby's head out of the water and her body floating near the surface. It is also very comfortable for her. Never leave her unattended in it.

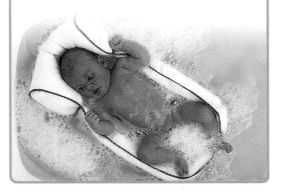

1 LOWER YOUR BABY INTO THE BATH

Unwrap your baby and cradle him in your arms, supporting his bottom half with one hand and his shoulders and head with the other. Lower him into the bath, bottom first.

2 RINSE HIS TORSO

Still supporting your baby behind his head and shoulders, gently splash water on to his chest and stomach. Smile and laugh to keep him amused.

3 WASH HIS UPPER BACK AND NECK

Sit your baby up, holding him under the armpit and supporting his chest across your arm. Rinse his upper back and the back of his neck.

4 RINSE HIS BOTTOM

Still supporting your baby across his chest, tip him forward, keeping his face clear of the water and using his knees for extra support. Rinse his lower back and bottom.

5 REMOVE HIM FROM THE BATH

Tip him back onto his bottom. Supporting his head and shoulders, hold him under the armpit and slide your other hand under his buttocks. Lift him out of the bath.

Drying your baby

Have a warmed towel ready to wrap your baby in. Soft cotton towels with integral hoods are specially made for babies and are snug and warm. You don't have to use one but it is a good idea to reserve towels for your baby's exclusive use.

As soon as you have removed your baby from the water, wrap him in the towel and cuddle him dry, smiling and talking with him all the while. This is a great opportunity to make your baby feel loved and secure.

Before you dress him, you should take care to ensure that all his skin creases, particularly those in his thigh and nappy area, are dry. Any moisture left is likely to cause soreness and irritation.

If you are going to use baby powder, shake it onto your hands first so that your baby does not inhale any; do not use any on the nappy area. You also need to avoid excessive dryness. Baby oil in the bath water, or baby lotion for delicate areas, will protect his sensitive skin, and you can use barrier creams to guard against nappy rash.

Remember that your baby's skin is very sensitive, so use a soft towel and gently pat him dry rather than rubbing.

SNUG, WARM AND RELAXED
Enjoy all aspects of your baby's bathtime. After a warm bath your baby will probably be at his most relaxed, so talk and sing to him as you pat him dry. These are precious moments so make sure you both enjoy them to the full.

1 Place your baby in the centre of the towel

As soon as you take him out of the bath, wrap your baby in a warm towel. Gently fold one side over him but take care not to cover his face, as this may cause him to panic and start crying.

2 Pat him dry all over

Fold both sides over so that he is completely wrapped up, and gently pat him dry. Pay particular attention to the skin creases around his legs, his nappy area, under his arms, and around his neck.

3 Keep your baby covered while you dress him

Begin to put on his clothes, keeping all exposed parts covered with the towel. This will help prevent him getting chilled. To be on the safe side, use a fresh clean towel for each bath.

Baby skin care

The two simple rules when buying baby skin care products are: choose products specifically made for babies; and avoid all products with fragrances and synthetic chemicals. Many products may smell gorgeous, but your baby's skin is extremely delicate and highly fragranced products may upset the balance of the natural oils found in her skin.

DAILY ROUTINES

In addition to changing and keeping your baby clean there are a number of other daily care routines you'll need to take into account. You will have to attend to your newborn's umbilical cord stump until it has dropped off and healed. Young babies have very sharp nails that should be kept short to prevent her scratching herself. Babies are often prone to cradle cap, which may need attention. Once your baby's teeth start to come through you'll want to begin tooth and gum care. Sleeping and playing are also important factors in your baby's life so putting her down to sleep – and keeping her amused while awake – will also be a part of your daily routine.

Taking care of the umbilical cord stump

The umbilical cord was your baby's lifeline while she was in your uterus, linking her to your bloodstream through the placenta. It provided her with oxygen, nutrients, antibodies and hormones, making her completely dependent on its supply.

When your baby takes her first breath, two momentous changes happen in seconds – her lungs inflate for the first time, and the blood flow is rerouted through the lungs, where previously it went through the umbilical cord. In an instant, your baby becomes able to survive independently.

Shortly after birth, the cord is clamped off and cut a few centimetres from the navel. There are no nerves in this area, so it is not a painful procedure for your baby. The cord will gradually shrivel up, turn black and, within about 10 days, fall off. Some parents – for sentimental or superstitious reasons – choose to keep the remnants of their baby's umbilical cord. In the meantime, however, it is susceptible to infection, particularly if it gets wet or dirty. As long as your baby's umbilical cord stump remains attached, try to leave it open to the air, as this will make it dry, heal and fall off more rapidly. While a slight discharge after the cord has withered is normal, call your doctor if the stump exudes pus or blood and the area around its base become inflamed. These symptoms probably indicate an infection.

UMBILICAL HERNIA
You may notice that when your baby cries her navel protrudes. This swelling is called an umbilical hernia and is very common among young babies.

Newborn babies have an opening in their abdominal walls through which blood vessels extend to the umbilical cord. After the cord is cut, stomach muscles grow and encircle the navel, but sometimes not completely. When your baby cries she puts pressure on these weak abdominal muscles, causing the intestines to push through to beneath the surface of her navel. The resulting bulge can be very small or the size of a golf ball. Surgery is not usually necessary as the opening generally closes up by itself after a year or two.

1 EXPOSE THE STUMP TO THE AIR

The stump will dry and heal much faster if you expose it to air as much as possible. In particular, don't cover it with plastic pants and nappies and, if it does get wet, make sure it is thoroughly dried.

2 CLEANING THE STUMP

Your midwife will advise you on what to use to clean your baby's cord stump. Using clean cotton wool, moistened as recommended, gently wipe the stump, the area around it, and the crevices of the navel. Make sure you dry the area gently.

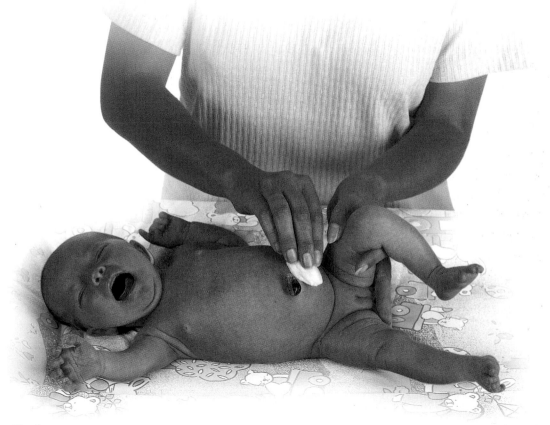

3 AFTER THE STUMP HAS FALLEN OFF

There may be a few spots of blood, and the wound will continue to heal. You should clean and dry it daily until the area is completely healed.

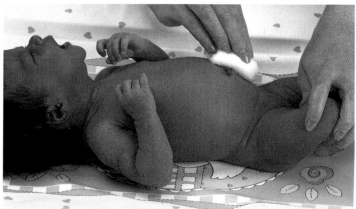

Caring for your baby's hair and nails

Some babies are born with a full head of hair, some have a sparse covering. Thick or thin, newborn hair is invariably shed after a couple of weeks – often a cause of concern for parents, but perfectly normal. Your baby may also have a covering of downy body hair, known as lanugo – this, too, will rub off within a couple of weeks.

Your baby's hair will need only simple care at first – wipe it down with a damp cloth or sponge (see page 64), and brush it through with a soft brush. Do not use a comb as it could catch on the scalp and cause your baby harm. Your young baby's head is particularly sensitive due to the soft areas known as the fontanelles (see box). Don't be afraid of handling your baby's head though: simply ensure that any contact with it is carried out with the utmost care.

Gentle washing and brushing of your baby's hair should also guard against cradle cap (see page 63).

A newborn's nails are often quite long and you should trim them to stop him scratching himself. Use an emery board to do this. Cutting with scissors can risk tearing the skin, which is not only uncomfortable for your baby but could also lead to infection. Alternatively, you can gently nibble off the nails – your mouth is more sensitive than a pair of scissors. Soft mittens on your baby's hands will prevent him scratching himself or irritating a dry skin condition.

Toenails tend to grow more slowly than fingernails but often excess skin encroaches on to the nail bed, making toenails difficult to trim. To avoid catching your baby's skin, file toenails straight across. If you do draw some blood, blot with a tissue then dab some antiseptic ointment onto the area.

The fontanelles

When your baby is born, the bones of his skull will not be entirely fused together, leaving small soft patches on the top of his head. These are known as the fontanelles. While you should obviously be careful around these, since they are spots where your baby's brain is vulnerable, they are covered with a tough membrane, so you don't have to avoid them altogether. Simply wash and dry over them gently, as you would the rest of your baby's skin. They won't knit together entirely until he is about two years old.

SLOWLY DOES IT
The idea of using scissors anywhere near your baby's fingers and toes can be daunting for parents. But if you have the right equipment and approach these tasks gently, your confidence will soon grow.

HAIR

USE A SOFT BRUSH

Your baby's head and scalp are very sensitive, so
always use a soft brush on your baby's hair. Treat
cradle cap by massaging baby oil into the scalp,
leave overnight and, using the soft brush, brush
off the scales the following morning.

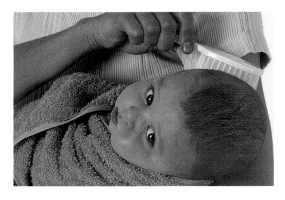

Infants' nails

You can cover your young baby's hands
with a pair of soft mittens to prevent her
scratching herself or irritating any dry
skin condition she may have.

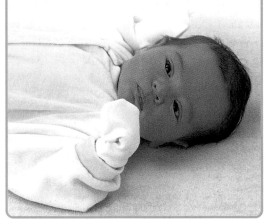

NAILS

TRIMMING YOUR BABY'S NAILS

Use baby scissors or baby nail clippers when
trimming nails. The scissors
have rounded edges –
because even the
sleepiest baby can
make a sudden move
that could cause you
to falter if you use
sharp, pointed scissors.
Trim finger- and
toenails after a bath,
when they are at their
softest, and cut them
straight across,
leaving no
ragged edges.

USING AN EMERY BOARD

Sit your baby comfortably in your lap so you can
hold her securely. Use one hand to hold her
fingers steady and the other to gently file along
the natural line with an emery board. Go slowly
and be as gentle as possible.

Teething

Your baby's first set of teeth are known as milk, primary or deciduous teeth. They amount to 20 in total and are usually all in place by the time your baby is two and a half years old. First teeth are very white which is one reason they are known as milk teeth.

At about six years of age your child will start to lose these teeth. They will gradually be replaced by a permanent set of 32 teeth.

Although the milk teeth are not permanent they are very important because they allow your baby to chew his food and help him to learn to speak correctly. Most importantly, they retain the space necessary for the permanent teeth.

Teeth are forming under the gums even before your baby is born and sometimes babies can be born with a milk tooth already in place. If this happens to your baby a paediatrican will check to see if it is securely fixed; if it is wobbly or if it interferes with breastfeeding it may have to be removed.

The first tooth usually appears at around five or six months of age but this can vary a great deal – anything between three to 12 months. The signs of teething will become apparent a few weeks before you see the first tooth. Your baby may start to drool a great deal and become irritable as the teeth cut through his gums.

OLD WIVES' TALES

Fever, vomiting and diarrhoea are not signs of teething – even though some parents may think they are. These symptoms could be signs of serious illness in your baby and should always be investigated by your doctor.

TEETHING RINGS

These special rubber rings often contain a gel that you can make cool by placing it in the refrigerator for a few hours. Your baby can put the teething ring in his mouth to massage and relieve any soreness around his gums.

When teeth appear

Teeth usually erupt in pairs from the front of the mouth to the back, the bottom pair arriving a couple of months before the corresponding top pair. Although the age at which babies begin to teethe and the rate at which it proceeds differ greatly, the first teeth that are likely to appear are (1) the lower central incisors followed by (2) the upper central incisors. Then (3) the upper lateral incisors (which sit either side of the central teeth) appear, followed by (4) the lower lateral incisors.

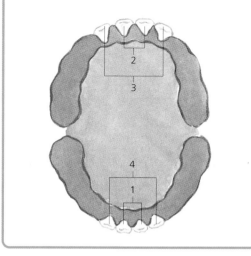

DROOLING

Your baby will put his fingers, sometimes even his whole fist, into his mouth; this may be because he is teething and wants to relieve any tingling pain. Too much drooling can lead to a rash around your baby's chin and lips so make sure you wipe away any saliva. If a rash develops, apply a small amount of barrier cream to the area.

BITING

Though many mothers successfully continue to breastfeed when their babies have teeth, it is important to teach your baby not to bite. Try immediately removing the breast so that your baby learns that biting interrupts feeding.

HARD FOODS

A firm piece of bread, a roll or a breadstick may help relieve any gum soreness. Any bits that break off will soften so your baby can swallow them without harm. You can buy special gluten-free baby rusks or teething biscuits for your baby to gnaw on, but check that these are not high in sugar, which can lead to tooth decay.

Caring for your baby's teeth

Once your baby starts to teethe it is a good idea to get into a daily routine of tooth and gum care. If your baby has just one or two teeth you can add a drop of toothpaste to a clean handkerchief or small piece of gauze cloth and use this to wipe them. Use specially manufactured baby toothpastes, which contain low levels of fluoride. Avoid those that contain added sugar to make them more palatable. The sugar will only encourage plaque. The general rule is to use a small smear of toothpaste for babies and children up to five years old. If you can, discourage your baby from swallowing toothpaste.

When your baby has more than a few teeth you should start using a soft, baby toothbrush. Your baby will not be able to clean her teeth properly for a few years yet, so you will have to take responsibility for this. Your baby will enjoy imitating you, however, so let her have her own brush to play with while she watches you brush your teeth. You

Fluoride

Fluoride is a mineral that can help to fight tooth decay. It comes from a number of different sources including toothpaste and drinking water. If you are unsure about using fluoride toothpaste ask your health visitor, dentist or doctor for advice.

should brush your baby's teeth every morning and every night before she goes to bed.

As well as daily cleaning you should limit the amount of sugary foods in your baby's diet. Never put your baby to bed with a bottle or let her suck endlessly on a bottle filled with milk or juice, as her teeth will be bathed in sugary fluid, which will encourage tooth decay. On the other hand, give her plenty of raw fruit and vegetables, which are naturally sweet and good to gnaw on.

Check frequently for signs of tooth decay and if you see any white, yellow or brown spots on the teeth contact your dentist. After the age of two, when most of your child's milk teeth will have erupted, you should take her for regular dental check-ups.

EARLY TOOTH CARE
Healthy milk teeth are essential for the proper development of your baby's jaw and later permanent teeth, so you should start caring for her first teeth even before they are visible.

Tooth safety

Hard, sharp toys can damage a baby's teeth and gums. Only let your baby chew on suitably soft but firm objects.

CLEAN ONE OR TWO BABY TEETH WITH A CLOTH

Gently wipe your baby's teeth and gums with a piece of gauze to get rid of the plaque, bacteria and acid that cause tooth decay. You can also use cotton buds, if you like.

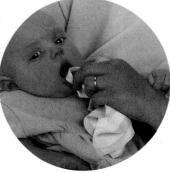

BRUSH YOUR BABY'S TEETH DAY AND NIGHT

Sit your baby on your lap with her back against you and carefully brush her teeth and gums. A gentle up and down motion will get rid of any plaque. Be careful when brushing the back of her mouth as your child might be frightened of gagging. Try and develop a routine of brushing in the morning and last thing at night.

Choosing a toothbrush

There is a wide variety of children's toothbrushes on the market. A brightly coloured one will appeal to your child – and may encourage her to use it.

Choose a toothbrush with soft, rounded bristles and change it every six to eight weeks, even if it doesn't look worn, because bacteria from your baby's mouth will accumulate on the brush.

Putting your baby down to sleep

Provided that she is not too cold or hungry, your newborn baby may sleep for 60 per cent of the time. Her readiness to sleep any time and any place can be a distinct advantage – until your baby has a regular night-time routine, you will be able to go out in the evenings and take your baby with you. It might, therefore, be advisable to buy something portable as a first bed – a carry cot, Moses basket or car seat with handles.

Your baby will sleep outside with no problem; just make sure that she is protected from draughts, biting insects and direct sunlight. When inside, check that the room's temperature is between 16 and 20°C. You may want to use a baby listening device to keep a check on her if she is in a separate room.

SUDDEN INFANT DEATH SYNDROME

SIDS (also known as cot death) is every parent's nightmare. Thanks to a number of recent studies, a good deal is now known about how to avoid the risk factors that predispose children to become victims.

Most important is your baby's sleeping position. You should always put your baby down to sleep on her back, with her feet touching the foot of her cot. This factor alone resulted in a halving of the rate of cot death in Britain in the year it was first publicized. Another important risk factor is smoking – both during and after pregnancy. Exposure to one parent's smoke doubles the risk of a baby dying of SIDS. Don't let anyone smoke in the same room as your baby and don't burn incense in your baby's room.

SIDS is more common in winter, probably as a result of babies becoming overheated or overwhelmed by heavy blankets. Use several light blankets instead of one heavy coverlet; they will give you finer control over your baby's temperature. Avoid insulators like cot bumpers, sheepskins and duvets. Don't cover your baby's head.

LISTENING DEVICE
Many parents like to use a sound monitor with two units – one positioned close to the baby and the other close to the parent – that can alert them to their baby's crying.

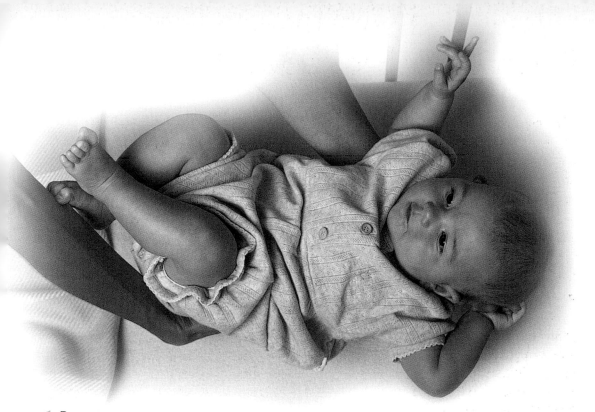

1 PLACE YOUR BABY ON HER BACK TO SLEEP

Always put your baby into her cot or pram on her back. Research into SIDS has shown that this is the most effective way of reducing your baby's risk, although the precise reason for this is still unknown.

Feet to foot

Position your baby so that her feet touch the foot of her cot, to prevent her from wriggling down under the covers. This way she can move as she wants to without the risk of getting the covers over her head. It can also help to reduce the risk of SIDS.

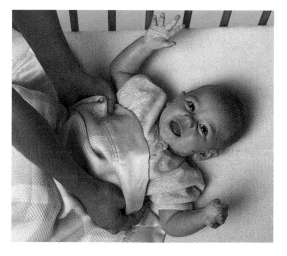

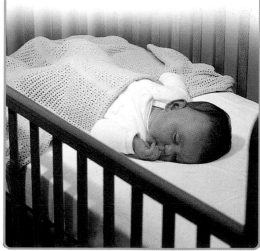

2 LIGHT CLOTHES, LIGHT COVERS

Do not overdress your baby. She should be lightly clothed for sleep. Always use light, cotton bedding and blankets. Make sure her head is not covered. Do not use duvets or sheepskins.

Sleeping through the night

As most parents will tell you, a lack of sleep is part and parcel of parenthood – especially in your baby's early weeks. It may, in fact, be months before your baby sleeps through the night. Below are some of the most frequently asked questions about babies' sleeping patterns, what you might expect to happen over the first few months of your baby's life, and how to establish a good night-time routine to maximize your chances of an undisturbed night.

Q **When will my baby start to sleep through the night?**

A Firstly, you must realize that, to a baby, 'sleeping through the night' means managing to sleep for a five-hour stretch. So if your baby already sleeps from midnight to five a.m., she's getting there! Most babies do not begin to establish this sort of regular sleeping pattern until they are about three or four months old (some much older), though some bottlefed babies may start sleeping for this long much earlier.

Establishing a bedtime routine in the early weeks will gradually help your baby recognize the various cues for going to sleep. Give her a bath to calm her down, and dress her in different clothes for bedtime than those she was wearing in the day. Feed her in her dimly lit and quiet bedroom. Give her a cuddle and put her to bed. Leave the room and let her settle herself down to sleep. The bath to bed process should take no more than 45 minutes to an hour.

Q **I read somewhere that by six months most babies are sleeping through the night, but my baby still wakes for feeds. Am I doing something wrong?**

A Babies love routine, and your baby may wake more as a matter of habit rather than hunger. Try stroking and comforting him (without picking him up from his cot) and you may think about offering him a dummy. You will find that when your baby's body clock becomes fully established he will go for longer stretches without food and begin to sleep more readily.

Make sure he is eating enough during the day and that his last feed is not too early. His bedtime milk (whether you are breast- or bottlefeeding) should fill and settle your baby down to sleep.

Q Why does my baby sleep more during the day than at night?

A Babies don't yet know the difference between night and day, so can get the two mixed up. To overcome this, treat daytime naps differently from your nightly bedtime routines: in the day, let your baby take his naps anywhere in the house, but at night make sure he's put to bed in his own room. Also, don't let your baby sleep for more than four uninterrupted hours during the day.

Finally, when your baby is awake during the day, play with him more, sing to him and massage him; but when it comes to bedtime, keep the lighting low and generally be quieter and more 'businesslike', so that your baby eventually learns the cues for going to sleep.

Q Should I go to my baby when she cries in the night?

A Even the experts disagree about the question of night-waking. Some parents find it very tough to 'impose' a routine on their babies, they can't bear to hear their infant cry at night, and reason that the crying baby must have some need to be fulfilled and that it's best to attend to her quickly. However, six months on, you may find that your quick reactions to her crying only reinforce your baby's expectations that you will always come when she wakes up in the night, and she will never learn to sleep through. Other parents leave their baby alone in the hope that she will cry herself to sleep, or try the technique of 'controlled crying' (see page 23). But this, too, can be distressing – for your baby and for you listening to her crying.

However if you do go in to your baby, try not to pick her up out of her cot, simply stroke her gently and talk to her quietly to reassure her; keep the room dark.

Q My newborn seems to sleep all the time – how much sleep do babies need?

A The amount of sleep babies need varies from child to child, so the following times are guidlines only. Newborn babies will probably sleep around 16–20 hours a day. This will gradually decrease until around six months, when your baby will average around 14 hours in a 24-hour period, including a couple of daytime naps of one or two hours each. By the age of two, most children sleep between 10 and 13 hours a day, including one daytime nap that can vary in length from 30 minutes to a couple of hours.

Amusing your baby

Your baby's play reflects her stage of mental, physical and sensory development. At first she will enjoy looking at moving objects and brightly coloured toys. By two months of age, as her coordination improves, she may begin swiping at things, particularly hanging mobiles. By three months your baby will be hitting and touching objects to get the feel of them – so she needs eye-catching objects that will stay within her reach. By five months she will want to put everything in her mouth, so choose your toys carefully – small and light enough for her to manipulate, but chunky enough to prevent choking.

Bear in mind that your baby has a very short attention span. Don't waste money on expensive toys that she will quickly lose interest in – simple household objects such as

keys or an empty box will do just as well. Also, remember that *you* are the most stimulating and responsive plaything your baby could want. Through simple play you can help your baby develop healthy emotional, physical and intellectual skills.

When you do buy toys, choose brightly coloured ones that make noises; these will more easily capture a young baby's interest. Interactive toys – with moving parts, levers and buttons – will exercise dexterity and teach her about cause and effect.

HANGING TOYS

Many seats or mats incorporate bright, dangling toys. Your baby will be enticed by these and will want to reach towards them, thus they will 'exercise' him, at the same time as providing visual stimulation.

A BASKETFUL OF TOYS

Babies have short attention spans so a large number of simple toys, rather than a few expensive ones, are preferable. Babies also enjoy putting objects into and taking them out of containers.

MAKE YOUR OWN FUN

Something as simple as a piece of cloth or a feather can engage your baby's interest, and teach her about texture and pliability, as well as heightening her hand-eye coordination.

MULTI-USE TOYS

Many toys can be used in more than one way. Spools, for example, can be placed one on top of another or threaded on a string and pulled.

INTERACTIVE TOYS

Once your child has a bit of dexterity she will enjoy shape sorters, pressing buttons, moving levers and imitating the actions of the adults around her.

CRAWL FOR IT

By about six months most babies enjoy lying prone. They can push up onto their arms and shift their weight to reach out and grasp toys. Try putting a favourite toy just out of your baby's reach and watch him go for it!

Parent and child activities

The times between those your baby spends sleeping, eating, crying and being washed and changed, can be the most rewarding for you both – playtime. In many ways, interacting with your child is more important than simply looking after his physical needs. It is vital for maintaining and enhancing the emotional bond between you, and can teach your baby about sociability and communication. Reading together will help promote your baby's speech and language development. Play will help your baby refine his movements, and improved coordination will assist in the development of his sensory integration and mental abilities. By responding to your baby's signals and encouraging his efforts, you build his confidence and self-belief, and reward and encourage his trust and love. You are your baby's first and most important teacher and play is a very important teaching tool.

ENCOURAGE HIS RESPONSE

Even a simple toy, such as a rattle or glove puppet, can teach your child a great deal about sound, movement and texture. Any response on his part should be rewarded with smiles and laughter.

Talk to your baby

One of the most important things you can do with your new baby is talk to him. The more you talk to your baby, the more you will enable him to become a good talker and a happy, confident child. When you are changing, bathing or feeding your baby, talk about what you have been doing throughout the day. Look at your baby when you talk to him and give him time to respond to your chatter with a smile – likewise, make sure that you respond to your baby's babbling.

Using toys

To make playtime more fun, give your baby's toys more character by providing movement and sound. This will help renew his interest in toys with which he may be bored.

Reading Together

Your baby will appreciate the sound of your voice and the idea of reading, even without total understanding. Point out and name objects and people in the story. As she gets older, your baby will be able to point to them on request.

Hide and seek

Your baby will enjoy watching you hide items under a towel or cushion, then retrieving them for you when you ask him where the 'lost' item is. Reward him with plenty of praise and cuddles.

Peek-a-boo

This game is fun for both parent and baby. Use exaggerated facial and vocal expressions as you cover your face and reveal it again to your baby. Even though you've 'disappeared' only momentarily, your baby will be happy to welcome you back.

SIGNS OF ILLNESS

In an emergency situation you should call for medical help on 999 immediately. An emergency is when your baby is unconscious or having difficulty breathing; is having convulsions; or is exhibiting unusual drowsiness, a blue or very pale colouration or a purple-red rash that does not fade when pressed, and abnormal floppiness. But there are some additional telltale signs that merit an immediate call.

The main warning symptoms are a raised or very low temperature – above 38°C (100.4°F) or below 35°C (95°F); extended diarrhoea (more than six hours); severe vomiting; loss of normally healthy appetite; listlessness; and prolonged crying that indicates to you that your baby may be in pain. Medical staff will appreciate any recorded observations about your baby's symptoms.

If you think your baby is ill

Only in rare circumstances will your doctor make a house call, so if you must make a surgery or hospital visit be prepared to take with you as much information as you can about your baby's condition, such as if and when he exhibited the symptoms listed above. A combination of symptoms is more serious than any one appearing singly.

A basic check to perform whenever you suspect your baby is sick is to take his temperature. Normal body temperature for a baby is 37°C (98.6°F). When the immune system is fighting infection this will rise, producing a fever, while a serious drop indicates hypothermia. Take the temperature more than once, since it may be fluctuating. Do not take your baby's temperature orally with a mercury thermometer in case he bites on and breaks the bulb – mercury is highly toxic. An accurate reading is given by an ear thermometer, though many parents prefer to use the underarm method. The least accurate is given by using a strip on the forehead.

A BABY'S PULSE

Parents are not normally required to take a baby's pulse except when recommended to do so by a doctor during illness.

The normal pulse rate for a young baby is quite high – between 100 and 160 beats per minute (bpm). A one-year-old's pulse slows to 100 to 120 bpm. A baby's pulse should be taken at the upper inner arm. Press your index and middle fingers gently against an artery until you can feel a beat. Then count the number of heart beats in 15 seconds and multiply by four to get the bpm.

Nursery care kit

It's a good idea to keep all the following items in one place in the nursery, so that you know exactly where to go when you need them. Useful items for your care kit include: a digital thermometer, medicine spoon/syringe, a nasal aspirator, scissors, tweezers, nail clippers, emery boards, bath temperature tester and a baby toothbrush.

TAKING AN UNDERARM TEMPERATURE

This is the recommended method for everyday use. You can use either a digital thermometer or a mecury one. Cradle your baby on your lap. Wipe dry his armpit, shake down the thermometer and put the bulb into the fold of his armpit. Hold his arm flat against his side, and leave for at least five minutes. The underarm is about 0.6°C (1°F) lower than the internal body temperature. The normal underarm temperature is about 36.4°C (98.4°F).

WHEN TO SEE THE DOCTOR

New babies can become ill very quickly, so it is important to be aware of the symptoms that could indicate illness. If a baby develops any of the following, or appears unwell, urgent medical advice is required.

- Paleness or a bluish colour around the mouth and on the face
- Fever with a temperature of 38°C (100.4°F) or more
- Body becomes floppy or stiff
- Eyes are pink, bloodshot, have a sticky white discharge, or eyelashes that stick together
- White patches in the mouth
- Redness or tenderness around the navel area
- Nose blocked by mucus, making it difficult for the baby to breathe while feeding
- Diarrhoea – more than six to eight watery stools per day
- Projectile vomiting
- Vomiting that lasts for six hours or more, or is accompanied by fever and/or diarrhoea
- Refusing to be fed
- Crying for unusually long periods
- Blood-streaked stools

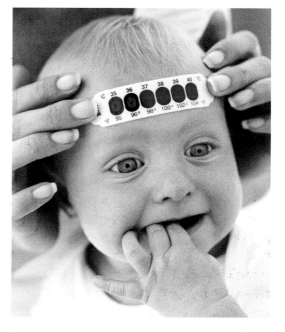

TAKING A TEMPERATURE USING A FOREHEAD STRIP

Hold the strip across your baby's forehead, with a finger on either end, for about a 15 seconds. Though easy to use, these strips are not very accurate, and are useful as a general guide only.

TAKING AN EAR TEMPERATURE

An ear thermometer works by measuring the temperature of the eardrum and surrounding tissues, to give a highly accurate and almost instantaneous reading.

When your baby is ill

After you have consulted with your doctor and determined the cause of your baby's illness, you will need to spend some time nursing your sick baby.

It may be distressing as a parent to witness your baby in physical discomfort but you can help by providing a warm and caring environment. Ill babies in particular will want to be in very close contact with their mothers and will seek a lot more physical attention. If you are breastfeeding, you may find your baby wanting to suckle simply for comfort.

If your baby has been vomiting, had diarrhoea or a high temperature you need to ensure she takes sufficient fluids to replace those she has lost. A high fever can be dangerous, so you should try and bring down your baby's temperature. Make sure she is not wearing too many clothes, and ensure a good supply of fresh air to her room. Try sponging your baby down with tepid water (see below right). As she cools down, pat her skin dry with the towel and cover her with a cotton sheet. Do not use cold water.

In general, you will be following your doctor's instructions, and your main task may be to give your baby prescribed medications.

IMMUNIZATION

While the antibodies your baby has picked up from you through the placenta and breastfeeding will help her fight off many infections, there are a number of common childhood diseases to which she will be susceptible. Several of these can be dangerous and even life-threatening, so you should make sure your baby is vaccinated against the major childhood illnesses. These are diphtheria, pertussis (whooping cough), polio, measles, mumps, rubella (German measles) and haemophilus infections (HIB), which can cause meningitis and other diseases. A DTP injection will also protect your baby against tetanus. Some of the immunizations are taken together and several involve a course of shots. All are injections except for polio. Your health visitor or doctor may suggest a dose of infant paracetamol post immunization to prevent fever.

GIVING MEDICINE BY ORAL SYRINGE
Cradle your baby in your arms and aim the tip of the syringe between her rear gums and cheek, avoiding the taste buds. Squirt the medicine slowly to avoid making her choke, and do not touch the back of the tongue with the syringe, since this could cause gagging.

Immunization schedule

These may vary according to local policy. Use this as a guide only and check with your family doctor.

DIPHTHERIA, TETANUS, PERTUSSIS (DTP)
Given at 2, 3 and 4 months (follow up for DTP at 3 to 5 years)
POLIO
Given at 2, 3 and 4 months (follow up at 3 to 5 years)
MEASLES, MUMPS AND RUBELLA (MMR)
Given any time between 12 to 15 months, but usually at 13 months
HAEMOPHILUS INFLUENZAE B (HIB)
Given at 2, 3 and 4 months
MENINGOCOCCAL C
Given at 2, 3 and 4 months

ADMINISTERING EYE DROPS
Swaddle your baby to prevent wriggling, and lay her on her back. Tilt her head to one side, with the affected eye nearest your leg. Taking care not to touch the eye with the dropper, pull down her lower eyelid and squeeze the drops between it and the eye. You may need help to hold her head steady.

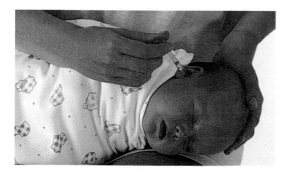

ADMINISTERING EAR DROPS
Lay your baby on her side, with the affected ear uppermost. You need to drop the medicine down the ear canal, so pull back the lobe to straighten the canal, and put the dropper close to her ear. Hold your baby steady while the drops sink in – you can use cotton wool to soak up any leaks.

GIVING MEDICINE BY DUMMY-STYLE SYRINGE
The nipple-shaped tip allows your baby to suck while you express the medicine. Hold your baby in your lap, supporting his head in the crook of your arm. Put the tip of the syringe in his mouth as you would with a bottle and slowly press the plunger.

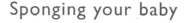

Sponging your baby

Bringing down your baby's high temperature will help him feel less irritable and more comfortable. Wrap him in a towel and sit him on your lap. Use a damp sponge soaked in boiled water cooled to a tepid temperature to wipe him down.

FIRST AID FOR BABIES

These basic instructions cannot substitute for proper first aid training, but they could help save your baby's life. Always call for help in an emergency so that someone can contact the emergency services on 999 while you attend to your baby. Priorities are to check that her airway is clear, that she is breathing, and that her pulse is above 60 beats/min (120 is normal for a baby). If you suspect a spinal injury, do not twist your baby's head or body, and make her lie still.

ELECTRIC SHOCK

A crawling baby may stick her fingers in an unprotected socket or chew on an electrical cord. A severe electric shock can stop her heart, interfere with breathing, cause shock, convulsions and severe burns. Your priority is to break the circuit your baby is forming without getting electrocuted yourself.

Turn off the current or disconnect the plug, if possible. If not, stand on some dry non-conductive material such as wood or plastic and push your baby away using a chair leg or broom handle. As a last resort, pull your baby away by her clothes. Check for burns; if present, cover with a sterile dressing or cling film.

If your baby is unconscious, place her in the position shown on page 94. If she is not breathing, you will need to perform rescue breaths and CPR (see page 95), if necessary.

POISONING

Take extra care to keep hazardous substances out of reach, and make sure that medicines have child-proof caps. Suspect poisoning if your baby exhibits signs of vomiting, dizziness, convulsions, unconsciousness, and burns or discoloration around the mouth.

Call 999 immediately. Try and find out what he took, how much and how long ago, so that you can inform the doctor or paramedics. Keep a sample of any vomit he produces – but don't try and make him sick. You can give him sips of water. If he is unconscious but breathing, put him in the position shown on page 94.

If your baby is not breathing, check for any obstructions in his mouth (see opposite), then give rescue breaths (see page 95).

BLEEDING

Severe blood loss could send your baby into shock (see page 94), and must be dealt with promptly. The basic rules are to apply direct pressure to the wound and raise the injured part above the level of the heart.

Lay your baby down and keep the injured part raised. If something is in the wound apply pressure on both sides, but do not remove the foreign body. Expose the wound by cutting away clothing, if necessary, and apply pressure with a clean dressing.

For a severe wound (e.g. one that is spurting blood, indicating that an artery is cut) apply pressure for at least 10 minutes, then put on a pressure bandage. If blood seeps through, do not replace the dressing but wrap more gauze around the first dressing.

CHOKING

If you suspect your baby is choking but she can still cry and cough, check her mouth, being careful not to push the obstruction further down her throat. Then pat her back gently. Only attempt the sequence below if she is conscious but cannot cry, cough or breathe, or if she is making high-pitched noises and is coughing very weakly.

If you do the following but still cannot feel a pulse, you must be prepared to perform CPR (see page 95).

1 GIVE FIVE BACK BLOWS
Lay your baby face down along your forearm with her head low and support her back and chin. Give up to five sharp back slaps between her shoulder blades. Check her mouth and very carefully remove any obvious obstruction, using one finger.

2 GIVE FIVE CHEST THRUSTS
If she still doesn't cry, turn her onto her back and give up to five chest thrusts. Push downwards on her breastbone, one finger's breadth below the nipple line, with two finger tips, at a rate of one every three seconds. Once again, check her mouth and remove any obvious obstructions. Do not feel blindly down her throat. Repeat the five back blows and five chest thrusts one to three times and, if you have not already done so, dial the emergency services. Repeat these steps until the object is coughed up, she becomes unconscious, or professional help arrives.

IF YOUR BABY LOSES CONSCIOUSNESS

Place your baby on her back on the floor and perform a foreign body check.

Place your baby onto a firm surface and open the airway, by placing one hand on her head and tilting it back slightly. Without feeling blindly down the throat, carefully remove any obvious obstruction from the mouth. Lift the chin using one finger

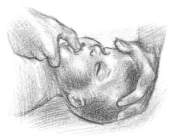

and check for your baby's breathing by listening for sounds of breathing, feeling for breath on your cheek and looking along her chest for movement.

IF YOUR BABY REMAINS UNCONSCIOUS AND NOT BREATHING

Open the airway by tilting her head back slightly and give two effective rescue breaths (see page 95) by sealing your lips tightly around her mouth and nose and breathing into the lungs until the chest rises. If the chest doesn't rise, perform CPR (see page 95) for one minute. Call an ambulance. Continue with CPR until your baby moves or help arrives.

SHOCK

Blood pressure drops dangerously low during this life-threatening condition. Warning signs are cold, sweaty skin; a greyish tinge around the lips and nails; shallow breathing and unconsciousness.

Call for emergency help immediately. Lay your baby on a coat or blanket, turn her head to the side, in case she vomits, and raise her feet above the level of her heart. Loosen any clothing and keep her warm but not hot. Check her breathing and pulse frequently. If breathing stops, perform rescue breaths and CPR, if necessary.

HOLDING AN UNCONSCIOUS BABY

If your baby is unconscious but breathing, and shows no signs of fracture, hold her in this modified recovery position until help arrives.

Cradle her in your arms with her head tilted downwards. This keeps her airway open and allows liquids to drain from her mouth.

RESCUE BREATHS AND CPR

A variety of accidents and emergency situations can cause your baby to fall unconscious and stop breathing.

If you find your baby lying still and suspect something is wrong, yell for help so another adult can contact the emergency services. You must resuscitate your baby if she is not breathing. If you are alone, begin resuscitating your baby but after one minute, ring the emergency services, while maintaining resuscitation.

Check for unconsciousness by tapping or scratching the soles of your baby's feet and calling her name. If she doesn't respond, turn her on to her back immediately. Try to roll your baby as a unit to prevent making any injuries worse. Support her all along the length of her body as you turn her on to her back. You then should perform rescue breathing and, if necessary, CPR.

IF YOUR BABY SHOULD VOMIT

Quickly turn your baby's head and body to the side, wiping away any vomit to ensure it doesn't get into her lungs. Continue artificial ventilation.

DROWNING

A baby who slips under the water in a bath – even if only two centimetres or so of water covers his mouth and nose – may drown in a couple of minutes.

If you find your baby in water, lift him out immediately and hold him so his head is lower than his body. This will help prevent water, or vomit if he throws up, getting into his lungs. If he is unconscious but still breathing, hold him as shown on the left, while you call the emergency services. If he is not breathing you must give rescue breaths and CPR, if necessary. Water in the lungs will mean you will have to breathe more firmly than usual to get the lungs inflated.

Rescue breathing

1 Open the airway and check for breathing

Gently supporting her forehead with one hand, place a finger (not the thumb) of your other hand under her jaw. Tilt her head

gently back by lifting the chin gently. See if you can detect any movement in the chest or feel any breath against your cheek.

2 Give two to five slow breaths

If there is no breathing, open your mouth wide and take a breath. Cover your baby's nose and mouth with your mouth and slowly breathe out for one to two seconds. Look to make sure her chest rises when you breathe into her and watch to see her

chest fall when you stop. Repeat until two effective breaths are given.

3 Look for signs of circulation

To see if your baby's heart is beating, look, listen and feel for breathing, coughing, movement or any other signs of life. If breathing starts, hold her in the recovery position. For a baby up to the age of one, cradle her in your arms so she is facing you with her head tilted slightly downwards (see page 94). If her chest doesn't rise and there is no breath, begin Cardiopulmonary Resuscitation (CPR).

CPR (Cardiopulmonary resuscitation)

1 Locate the compression point

Place your baby flat on her back. Hold her forehead with one hand and position the index finger of the other just under the midpoint of an imaginary line running

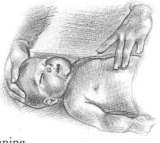

between her nipples. Place the next two fingers underneath. Raise the index finger. You should be on the bottom of the breastbone.

2 Compress the chest five times

Using your two fingers and bending your elbow, push down sharply 1½ to 2½ cm (½ to 1 inch), then release. Use a steady down and up pace. Give five compressions in three seconds (100 every minute).

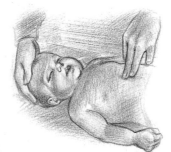

3 Give one slow breath

After five compressions, check the mouth and give one slow breath lasting one to two seconds. Repeat the five compressions. Alternate one breath and five compressions, checking the mouth after every set until help arrives. If the baby's colour improves or there are signs of circulation, stop the compressions but continue ventilation until your baby starts breathing or help arrives.

INDEX

ACKNOWLEDGEMENTS

Carroll and Brown would like to thank:

Paula Bell & Kashmir Randhawa, health visitors, for their expert baby health advice.

Alison Mackonochie for editorial work.

Mike Good, Debi Treloar, Jules Selmes, Roger Dixon for photography.

John Geary for illustrations.

Mamas and Papas for items featured in photographs.
www.mamasandpapas.com

JoJo Maman Bebe for items featured in photographs.
www.JoJoMamanBebe.co.uk